Trends in Landbird Abundance at Channel Islands National Park, 1993-2009

Natural Resource Technical Report NPS/CHIS/NRTR—2011/507

Timothy J. Coonan

National Park Service
Channel Islands National Park
1901 Spinnaker Drive
Ventura, CA 93001

Robert C. Klinger

U.S. Geological Survey – Biological Resources Division
Yosemite Field Station - Bishop Office
568 Central Avenue
Bishop, California 93514

Linda C. Dye

National Park Service
Channel Islands National Park
1901 Spinnaker Drive
Ventura, CA 93001

November 2011

U.S. Department of the Interior
National Park Service
Natural Resource Stewardship and Science
Fort Collins, Colorado

The National Park Service, Natural Resource Stewardship and Science office in Fort Collins, Colorado publishes a range of reports that address natural resource topics of interest and applicability to a broad audience in the National Park Service and others in natural resource management, including scientists, conservation and environmental constituencies, and the public.

The Natural Resource Technical Report Series is used to disseminate results of scientific studies in the physical, biological, and social sciences for both the advancement of science and the achievement of the National Park Service mission. The series provides contributors with a forum for displaying comprehensive data that are often deleted from journals because of page limitations.

All manuscripts in the series receive the appropriate level of peer review to ensure that the information is scientifically credible, technically accurate, appropriately written for the intended audience, and designed and published in a professional manner. This report received informal peer review by subject-matter experts who were not directly involved in the collection, analysis, or reporting of the data.

Views, statements, findings, conclusions, recommendations, and data in this report do not necessarily reflect views and policies of the National Park Service, U.S. Department of the Interior. Mention of trade names or commercial products does not constitute endorsement or recommendation for use by the U.S. Government.

This report is available from **National Park Service Mediterranean Coast Network** (http://science.nature.nps.gov/im/units/medn/reports/index.cfm) and the Natural Resource Publications Management website (http://www.nature.nps.gov/publications/nrpm/).

Please cite this publication as:

Coonan, T. J., R. C. Klinger and L. C. Dye. 2011. Trends in landbird abundance at Channel Islands National Park, 1993-2009. Natural Resource Technical Report NPS/CHIS/NRTR—2011/507. National Park Service, Fort Collins, Colorado.

NPS 159/111616, November 2011

Contents

Contents (continued)

Figures

Figures (continued)

Figures (continued)

Tables

Abstract

Landbird monitoring began at Channel Islands NP in 1993, and the >18 years of data represent one of the longest-running landbird monitoring programs in the U.S. The program originally comprised non-randomly located line transects that cut through a number of habitat types, but, in response to a program review in 2000, the program switched to point counts along transects randomly located and stratified by habitat type. Perpendicular distance to birds was recorded under both phases, facilitating estimation of density via distance methods for those species with enough cumulative observations (>50) to construct detectability curves. Density estimation via distance methods provided trend data for 18 of the park's 44 breeding landbird species, and presence/absence data were available for 4 additional species. Density estimates were characterized by high inter-annual variability, but regression of density over time provided trend results for a number of species.

Western meadowlarks (*Sturnella neglecta*) and spotted towhees (*Pipilo maculatus*) increased after cattle were removed from Santa Rosa Island. The program also detected ecological changes during the period of island fox (*Urocyon littoralis*) absence from the wild; ground-nesting northern harriers (*Circus cyaneus*) began nesting on San Miguel and Santa Rosa Islands when foxes were in captivity, and populations of endemic song sparrows (*Melospiza melodia graminea*), orange-crowned warblers (*Vermivora celata sordida*) and Allen's hummingbirds (*Selasphorus sasin sedentarius*) increased and/or exhibited greater fluctuation when foxes were in captivity on San Miguel Island.

Rock wrens (*Salpinctes obsoletus*) and house finches (*Carpodacus mexicanus*) declined on San Miguel Island, and black phoebes (*Sayornis nigricans*) declined on Santa Rosa Island, for unknown reasons. American kestrels (*Falco sparverius*) declined on San Miguel and Santa Rosa Islands, and European starlings (*Sturnus vulgaris*) all but disappeared from the 4 park islands surveyed. Common ravens (*Corvus corax*) increased substantially on San Miguel Island likely due to changes in pinniped carcass availability. The methods were incapable of detecting trends for rare species such as the island loggerhead shrike (*Lanius ludovicianus anthonyi*), for owls, and for some large raptors such as red-tailed hawks (*Buteo jamsicensis*), eagles and peregrine falcons (*F. peregrinus*).

Investigation of habitat utilization via selectivity and diversity indices revealed complex patterns of habitat utilization for 15 species. Landbird diversity generally increased with increasing habitat diversity, with woodland, riparian, pine and chaparral habitat types having the greatest landbird use. Grasslands had surprisingly high species richness, perhaps due to sampling size but also to invasion of grass areas by native shrubs and relaxed niches for island species. In fact, few species were habitat specialists, and 13 of the 15 species analyzed showed preferences for ≥ 3 habitat types. Black phoebes and endemic horned larks (*Eremophila alpestris insularis*) had the most specialization, each strongly preferring one habitat type (riparian and grassland, respectively). Some species that occurred on multiple islands showed preferences for a greater number of habitat types on Santa Rosa Island than on smaller San Miguel and/or Santa Barbara Islands. For 5 of 9 species, densities from point counts were correlated with densities from line transects. Point count densities were generally higher than densities from line transects.

Acknowledgments

Landbird monitoring was conducted by a number of observers, most notably Greg Austin, Mitch Dennis, Kara Randall, Cedric Villasenor, Carlyn Greene, Andrea Lehotsky, Sara Hansen, Tessa Smith, Susan Coppelli, Julie Goldzman, Jen Savage and Helen Fitting. Paul Lukacs provided valuable advice regarding data analysis. We thank Rocky Rudolph for maps and other GIS products and analysis. This report was greatly improved by the critical review of Steve Fancy, Linnea Hall, Stacey Osterman-Kelm and Greg Kudray.

Introduction

Although landbirds are among the most conspicuous and diurnal of vertebrates, reported trends from longterm datasets are rare, perhaps due to the high variability produced by traditional monitoring methods, such as point counts, and differences in detectability among observers. Recent advances in distance-based sampling methods (Buckland et al. 2001) allow the development of density estimates with reasonable confidence intervals, by incorporating species and observer-specific detectability curves. We used such methods to analyze long-term trends in landbird populations at Channel Islands National Park (Fig. 1), where landbird monitoring has been conducted since 1993 as part of the park's long-term ecological monitoring program.

The avifauna of California's Channel Islands has long been of interest to both conservationists and researchers. Early investigations focused on classic island biogeographic theory and questions such as the rate of species turnover on nearshore islands (Diamond 1969, Lynch and Johnson 1974). Also, the islands' isolation from the adjacent mainland has resulted in an overall depauperate avifauna and the evolution of endemic forms. Forty-four landbird species are known to breed on the park islands (Table 1). Johnson (1972) reported that 13 breeding landbird taxa were endemic to the Channel Islands, and nine endemic bird taxa occur on the five park islands (Table 2). Several endemic taxa are currently of management concern. For example, the island scrub jay (see Table 1 for scientific names) is the only full landbird species designated as endemic on the Channel Islands. The species occurs only on Santa Cruz Island and recently underwent a population decline that focused attention on its current and future threats. Of greatest concern is potential vectoring of West Nile virus (WNV) to the island, which may occur if warming temperatures allow WNV-host mosquito species to establish on the islands (S. Morrison, The Nature Conservancy, pers. comm.). West Nile Virus causes high mortality in the jay's mainland relative, the western scrub jay. Another species, the island loggerhead shrike, is an endemic subspecies found on Santa Cruz and Santa Rosa Islands. It may currently be in decline on those islands, where it exists at very low numbers, and has presently been the object of intensive survey efforts.

Two introduced species currently breed or recently bred on the park islands. California quail were introduced to Santa Rosa Island during the historic ranching period. European starlings were not intentionally introduced, but recently occurred on Santa Rosa Island at the abandoned military base, and were once thought to be common or abundant residents on all islands (van Riper III et al. 1988, Jones et al. 1999).

In this report we analyze 17 years (1993-2009) of transect and point count data for trends. The National Park Service established a monitoring program for landbirds in 1988 as part of its long-term ecological monitoring program for the park (Davis et al. 1994). The objective of the landbird monitoring program was to be able to detect change in abundance and/or distribution of breeding landbirds in the park (van Riper III et al. 1988). The park's landbird monitoring program was originally established for San Miguel, Anacapa and Santa Barbara Islands, and a separate protocol was developed for the larger Santa Rosa Island in 1992 (Super et al. 1991). Landbird monitoring was never established by NPS for Santa Cruz Island, of which two-thirds is owned and managed by The Nature Conservancy (TNC) and the remainder by the NPS. However, TNC established 100 point count sites on Santa Cruz Island in the 1990s, and data

1

exist for a handful of years from those sites. Those data are not included in this analysis, since they do not include distance estimates, and so this report does not evaluate trends for the 9 landbird species within the park that breed only on Santa Cruz Island.

Table 1. Island-specific breeding status of landbirds known to breed at Channel Islands National Park. Data from Jones et al. (1999), Latta et al. (2005), and C. Drost, USGS-BRD, unpubl. data.

Common Name	Latin Name	SM[1]	SR	SC	AN	SB
Great blue heron	Ardea herodias		B[2]			
Golden eagle	Aquila chrysaetos		O	O		
Red-tailed hawk	Buteo jamaicensis	B	B	B	B	
Northern harrier	Circus cyaneus	O	O			
Bald eagle[3]	Haliaeetus leucocephalus		B	B	B	
Peregrine falcon	Falco peregrinus	B	B	B	B	B
American kestrel	Falco sparverius	B	B	B	B	B
California quail	Callipepla californica		B	B		
Mourning dove	Zenaida macroura		B	B		O
Barn owl	Tyto alba	B	B	B	B	B
Northern saw-whet owl	Aegolius acadicus			B		
Short-eared owl	Asio flammeus					B
Burrowing owl	Athene cunicularia					B
White-throated swift	Aeronautes saxatalis		B	B	B	
Anna's hummingbird	Calypte anna	B		B		
Allen's hummingbird	Selasphorus sasin	B	B	B	B	
Northern flicker	Colaptes auratus			B		
Acorn woodpecker	Melanerpes formicivorus			B		
Pacific-slope flycatcher	Empidonax difficilis		B	B	B	
Black phoebe	Sayornis nigricans	O	B	B		
Ash-throated flycatcher	Myiarchus cinerascens			B		
Horned lark	Eremophila alpestris	B	B	B		B
Barn swallow	Hirundo rustica	B	B	B	B	B
Island scrub-Jay	Aphelocoma insularis			B		
Common raven	Corvus corax		B	B		
Red-breasted nuthatch	Sitta canadensis			B		
Canyon wren	Catherpes mexicanus			O		
Rock wren	Salpinctes obsoletus	B	B	B	B	B
Bewick's wren	Thryomanes bewickii		B	B	B	
Blue-gray gnatcatcher	Polioptila caerulea			B		
Northern mockingbird	Mimus polyglottos		B	B		
Loggerhead shrike	Lanius ludovicianus		B	B		
European starling	Sturnus vulgaris		B			
Hutton's vireo	Vireo huttoni		B	B	B	
Orange-crowned warbler	Vermivora celata	B	B	B	B	B
Black-headed grosbeak	Pheucticus melanocephalus			B		
Rufous-crowned sparrow	Aimophila ruficeps			B	B	
Grasshopper sparrow	Ammodramus savannarum			B		
Song sparrow	Melospiza melodia	B	B	B		
Spotted towhee	Pipilo maculatus		B	B		
Chipping sparrow	Spizella passerina		B	B	B	

Table 1. Island-specific breeding status of landbirds known to breed at Channel Islands National Park. Data from Jones et al. (1999), Latta et al. (2005), and C. Drost, USGS-BRD, unpubl. data (continued).

Common Name	Latin Name	SM[1]	SR	SC	AN	SB
Western meadowlark	*Sturnella neglecta*	B	B	B	B	B
Lesser goldfinch	*Carduelis psaltria*	O	B	B		
House finch	*Carpodacus mexicanus*	B	B	B	B	
Total		16	29	39	15	11

[1] SM = San Miguel, SR = Santa Rosa, SC = Santa Cruz, AN = Anacapa, SB = Santa Barbara
[2] B = regular breeder, O = occasional breeder
[3] Bald eagles bred successfully on Santa Cruz in 2006, and have attempted breeding on Santa Rosa and Anacapa Islands in recent years

Table 2. Endemic landbird taxa at Channel Islands National Park (San Miguel, Santa Rosa, Santa Cruz, Anacapa and Santa Barbara Islands).

Species	Island form	Mainland form	Reference	Notes
Allen's hummingbird	*S. s. sedentarius*	*S. s. sasin*	Mitchell (2000)	*sedentarius* known also from Palos Verdes peninsula
Pacific-slope flycatcher	*E. d. insulicola*	*E. d. difficilis*	Lowther (2000)	
Horned lark	*E. a. insularis*	*E. a. actia*	Beason (1995)	21 subspecies recognized
Island scrub-jay	*A. insularis*	*A. californica*	Delaney and Wayne (2005)	Only island endemic which is full species; mainland form is western scrub-jay
Bewick's wren	*T. b. nesophilus*	*T. b. charienturus*	Kennedy and White (1997)	*T. b. catalinae* occurs on Santa Catalina Island
Loggerhead shrike	*L. l. anthonyi*	*L. l. gambeli*	Eggert et al. (2004)	*L. l. mearnsi* occurs on San Clemente Island
Orange-crowned warbler	*V. c. sordida*	*V. c. lutescens*	Gilbert et al. (2010)	*V. c. sordida* also occurs on s. California coast
House finch	*C. m. clementis*	*C. m. frontalis*	Hill (1993)	*clementis* occurs on southern islands, including Santa Barbara; house finches on northern islands are the mainland subspecies, *frontalis*
Rufous-crowned sparrow	*A. r. obscura*	*A. r. ruficeps*	Collins (1999)	
Song Sparrow	*M. m. graminea*	*M. m. heermanni*	Arcese et al. (2002)	Song sparrows on Santa Cruz are likely hybrids between *graminea* and *heermanni*

Note: Spotted towhees on Santa Rosa were formerly thought to be the San Clemente spotted towhee (*P. m. clementae*), which occurs on San Clemente and Santa Catalina (Johnson 1972), but are now thought to be of the mainland subspecies, *P. m. megalonyx* (Greenlaw 1996). Spotted towhees were extirpated on San Clemente by 1976 (Greenlaw 1996).

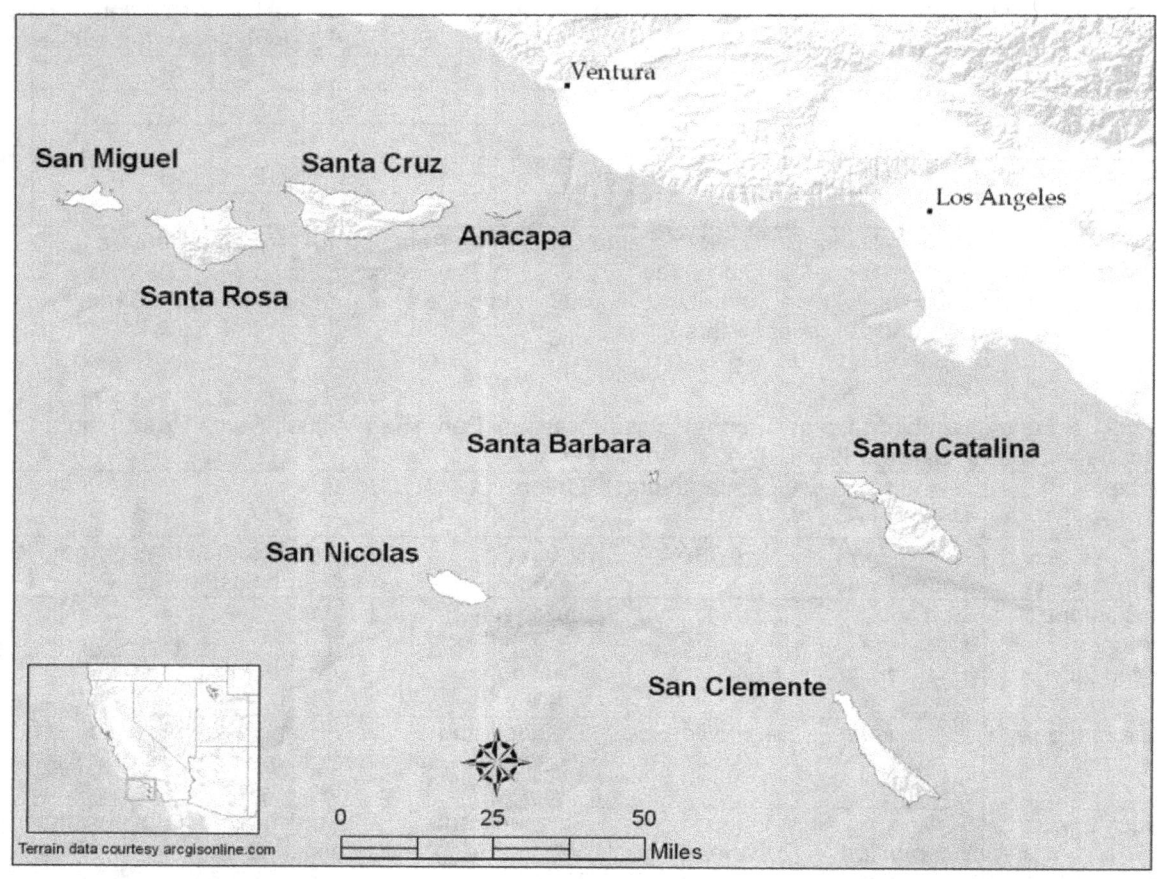

Figure 1. Channel Islands National Park comprises San Miguel, Santa Rosa, Santa Cruz, Anacapa, and Santa Barbara Islands.

Methods

Channel Islands National Park comprises 5 of the 8 Channel Islands which lie off the coast of southern California (Fig. 1). The park islands range in size from <3 km^2 (Anacapa and Santa Barbara Islands) to >200 km^2 (Santa Rosa and Santa Cruz Islands). The smaller islands are generally low in elevation and have little topographical relief; they are dominated by grass and shrub communities such as alien annual grasslands, *Isocoma* scrub, *Baccharis* scrub, giant coreopsis, lupine scrub, coastal bluff scrub and coastal sage scrub. The larger islands are topographically diverse and have either deep canyons draining a central massif (Santa Rosa) or a large central valley between two mountain ranges, the product of an east-west trending fault line (Santa Cruz Island). In addition to the previously mentioned grass and shrub communities, the larger islands also have extensive areas of chaparral, as well as several types of woodland (i.e., closed-cone pine, Torrey pine, oak, and ironwood).

The islands have a Mediterranean-type climate, characterized by warm, dry summers and cool winters, during which most precipitation occurs. Some precipitation also comes in the form of fog moisture in spring and summer, when a marine layer is pushed onshore by northwest winds. Consequently, islands at the western end of the chain, such as San Miguel, are cooler and moister than those to the southeast (Santa Barbara).

From 1993 through 2009 landbirds were surveyed on line transects and at point count sites (Figs. 2-5). The original landbird monitoring protocol developed for the park's long-term ecological monitoring program (van Riper et al. 1988) comprised line transects, along island trails, which crossed multiple habitat types. Each transect was monitored once annually, in the spring (March – April). An observer walked each transect between dawn and 10:00 a.m. and recorded the perpendicular distance from the transect midline to each bird or group of birds detected visually or aurally (i.e., by call or song). Transects were not surveyed if wind was greater than 10 knots or if it was raining at the time. The transects, which had been established on the three smallest park islands (San Miguel, Anacapa and Santa Barbara) were surveyed annually from 1993 through 2007, with a few exceptions (Table 3).

Point count sampling, rather than line transect sampling, was conducted on Santa Rosa Island, due to that island's varied topography and habitat diversity (Super et al. 1988). Transects of up to 20 point count stations, spaced ≥ 100 m apart, were established in different habitat types. Point count stations were surveyed in the spring (March – May) under the same environmental constraints as the line transect surveys. Staffing constraints prevented complete survey of Santa Rosa point count station transects in the 1990s (Table 4). At each point count site, after a settling period of ≥ 3 min, observers estimated the perpendicular distance from the point count center to each bird or group of birds detected by sight, call or song, for a 10-minute period.

Table 3. Years in which line transect surveys were conducted at Channel Islands National Park for landbird monitoring.

Island	Site	Length (km)	1993	1994	1995	1996	1997	1998	1999	2000	2001	2002	2003	2004	2005	2006	2007
AN	East Anacapa	3.5	X	X		X	X	X		X	X		X	X	X		
SB	Arch Point Loop	5.4	X	X	X	X	X	X		X	X	X	X	X	X		
SB	Canyons	2.5	X	X	X	X	X	X		X	X	X	X	X	X		
SB	Signal Peak Loop	6.3	X	X	X	X	X	X		X	X	X	X	X	X		
SM	Dry Lakebed	5.4	X	X	X		X	X	X	X	X	X	X	X	X	X	X
SM	Harris Point	1.6	X	X	X	X	X	X	X	X	X	X	X	X	X	X	X
SM	Nidever Canyon	1.4	X	X	X	X	X	X	X	X	X	X	X	X	X	X	X
SM	San Miguel Hill	2.3	X	X	X	X	X	X	X	X	X	X	X	X	X		
SM	Willow Canyon	3.0	X	X	X	X	X	X	X	X	X	X	X	X	X	X	X

*AN = Anacapa, SB = Santa Barbara, SM = San Miguel

A program review conducted by the USGS Biological Resources Division (McEachern 2000) recommended shifting to point count sampling with randomly located sites, stratified by habitat type, on all islands. Consequently, a total of 226 point count sites were established: 8 on Anacapa, 33 on Santa Barbara, 40 on San Miguel, and 145 on Santa Rosa (Table 4). For a plot of 50 m radius at each site the percent cover of different vegetation types was visually estimated, and the dominant type was identified as habitat type for that point. On the smaller islands (Anacapa, Santa Barbara, and San Miguel), the number of point count sites was determined by the maximum number that could be randomly located with trap spacing of at least 250 m. Due to the small size of Santa Barbara Island, its point count sites were established on a grid (Fig. 2) so that a sufficient number of sites could be located while maintaining adequate space between sites. On Santa Rosa (216 km^2), many point count sites were located on transects of 3-5 sites to reduce travel time. Monitoring at the new point count sites began in 2002 with a period of overlap with line transect monitoring of at least 3 years on each island (Tables 3 and 4) before shifting completely to point counts.

a)

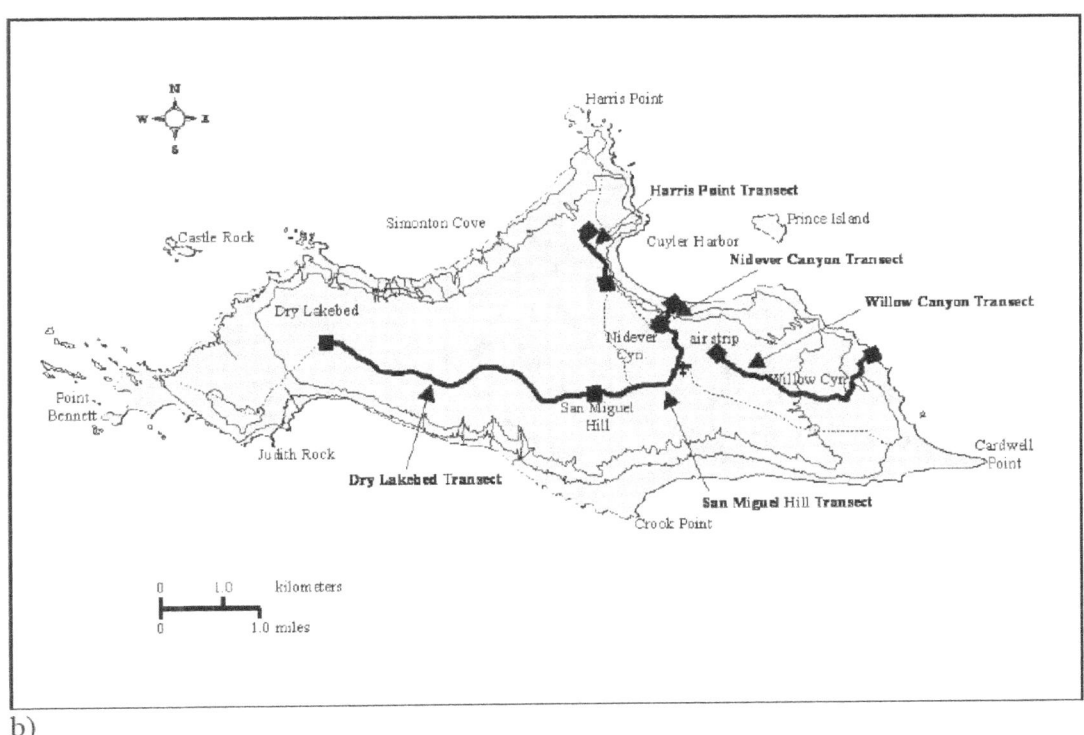

b)

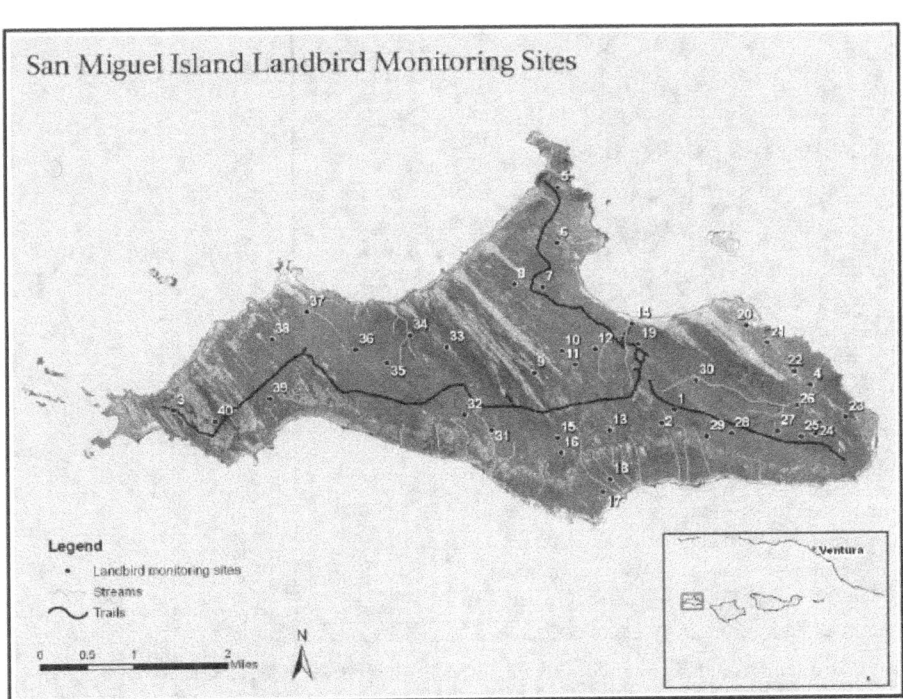

Figure 2. Locations of line transects (a) from the original park landbird monitoring protocol (van Riper et al. 1988), and point count sites (b) on San Miguel Island, Channel Islands National Park.

a)

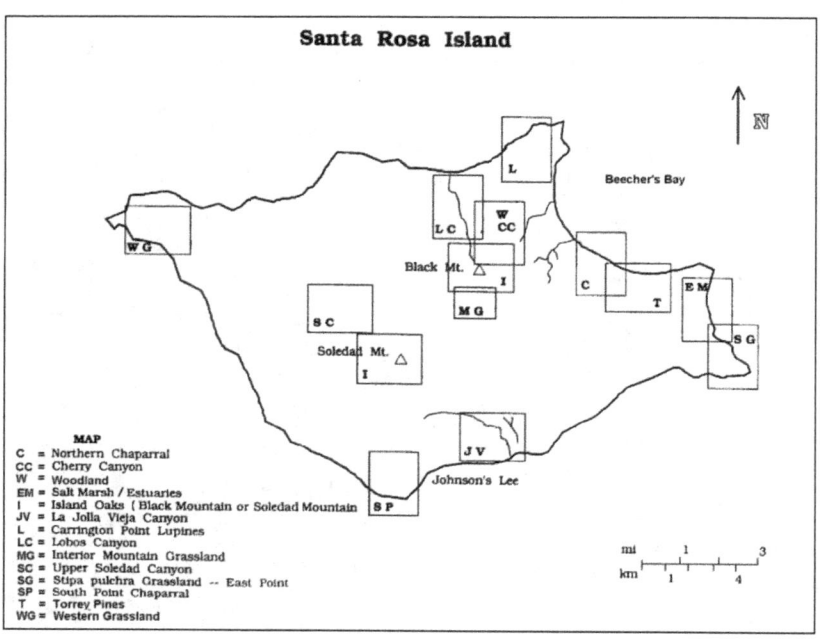

Santa Rosa Island

Beecher's Bay

Black Mt.

Soledad Mt.

Johnson's Lee

MAP
C = Northern Chaparral
CC = Cherry Canyon
W = Woodland
EM = Salt Marsh / Estuaries
I = Island Oaks (Black Mountain or Soledad Mountain
JV = La Jolla Vieja Canyon
L = Carrington Point Lupines
LC = Lobos Canyon
MG = Interior Mountain Grassland
SC = Upper Soledad Canyon
SG = Stipa pulchra Grassland -- East Point
SP = South Point Chaparral
T = Torrey Pines
WG = Western Grassland

mi   1   3
km 1   4

b)

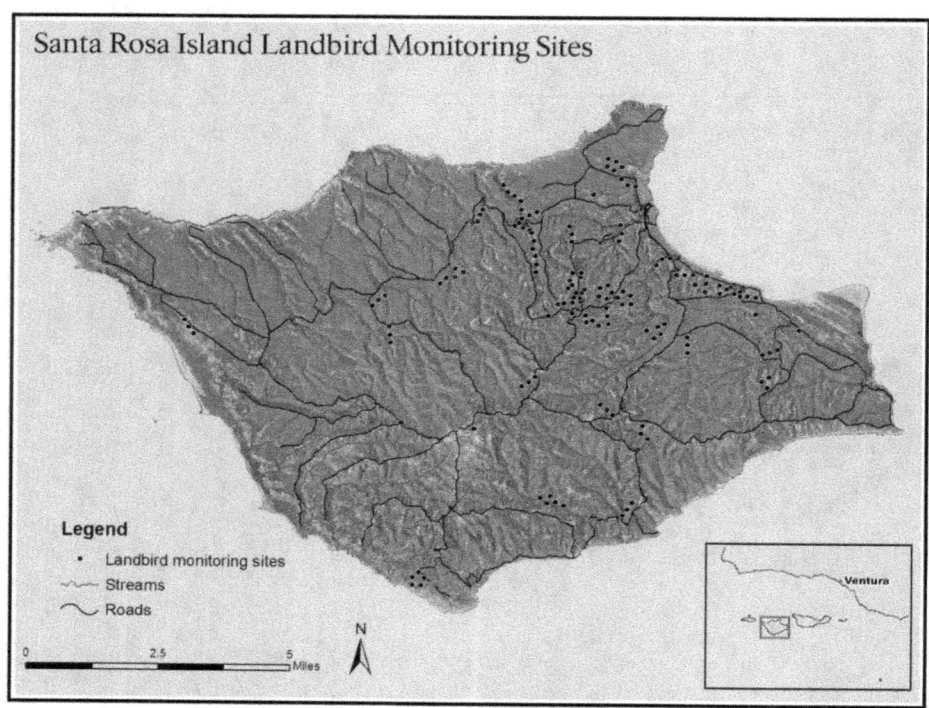

Santa Rosa Island Landbird Monitoring Sites

Legend
• Landbird monitoring sites
⌇ Streams
⌇ Roads

0   2.5   5
Miles

N

Ventura

Figure 3. Locations of original point count sites (a) from the legacy Santa Rosa Island landbird monitoring protocol (Super et al. 1991) and new point count sites (b) on Santa Rosa Island, Channel Islands National Park. In (a), boxes denote general areas where point count transects were established.

8

a)

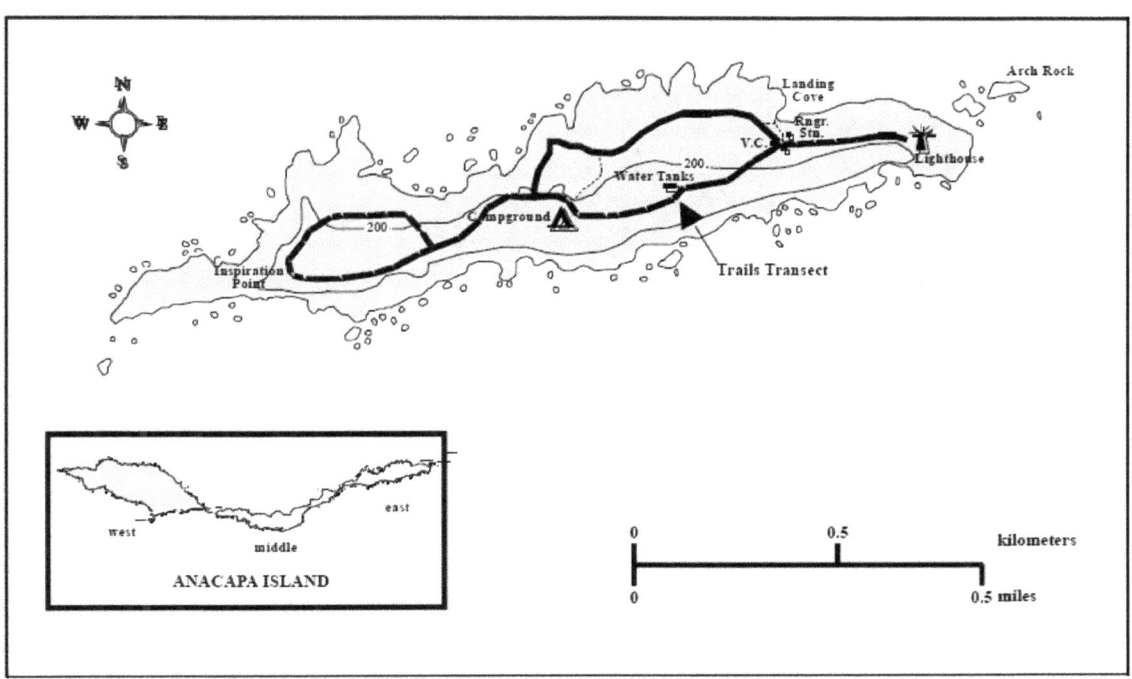

b)

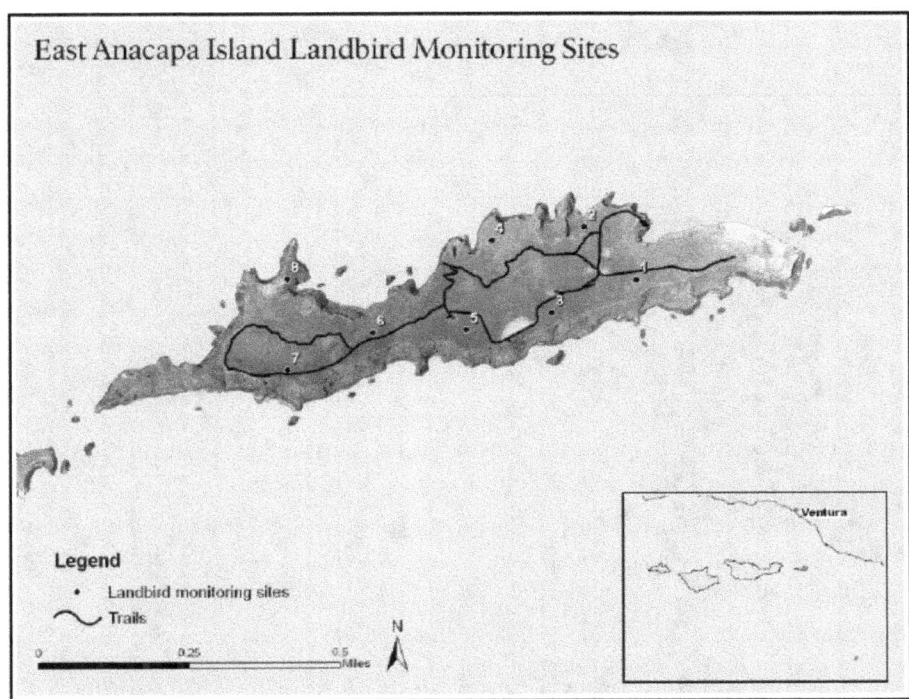

Figure 4. Locations of line transects (a) from the original park landbird monitoring protocol (van Riper et al. 1988) and point count sites (b) on Anacapa Island, Channel Islands National Park.

a)

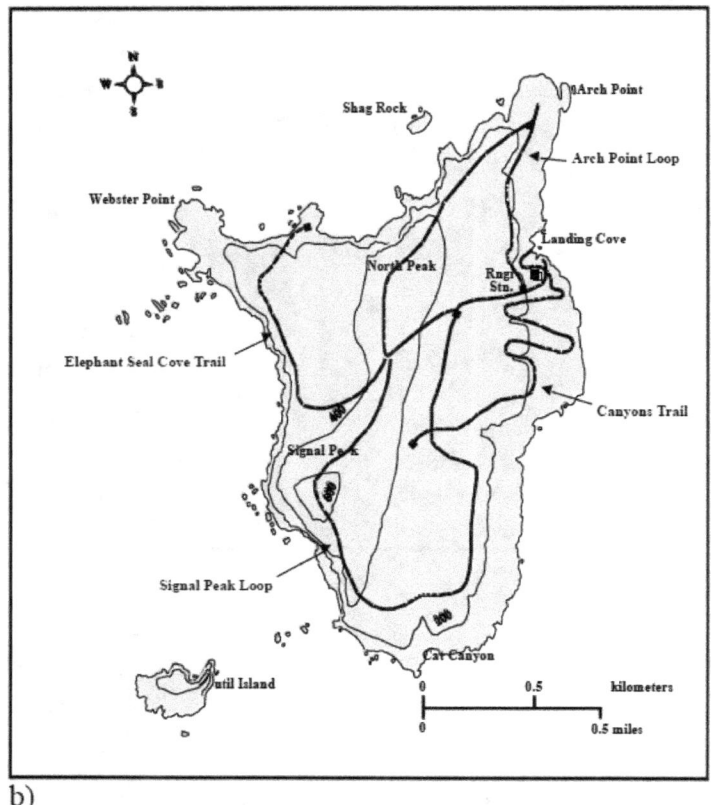

b)

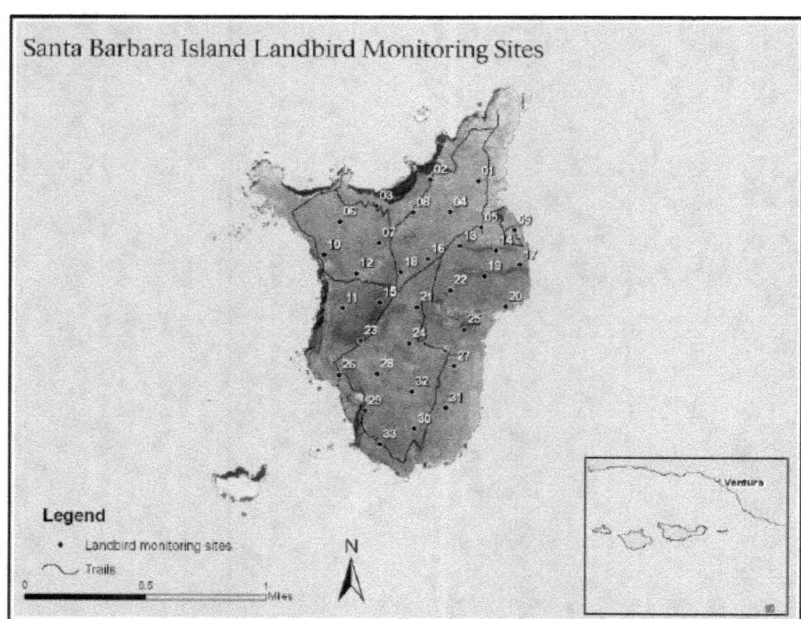

Figure 5. Locations of line transects (a) from the original park landbird monitoring protocol (van Riper et al. 1988) and point count sites (b) on Santa Barbara Island, Channel Islands National Park.

Under each method, observers recorded perpendicular distance to all birds detected by visual or auditory cue, allowing estimation of density by program Distance (ver. 4.1; Thomas et al. 2003). Twenty of the park's 44 breeding species of landbirds had a sufficient number of detections (>50; Buckland et al. 2001) on either line transects or point counts to allow construction of detectability curves by program Distance (Table 5). For those species we estimated density from either line transect or point-count data using global detectability with observer as a covariate, to account for the multiple observers who conducted monitoring over the 15-year period. In cases where the model with observer as covariate failed to run (see Table 6), we used a model that did not include observer as a covariate. For analyses with observer as a covariate, we tested the half-normal estimator with both the cosine and Hermite modifiers, and the hazard estimator with the simple polynomial modifier. For analyses without observer as covariate, we were able to test one additional estimator, the uniform, with both the cosine and simple polynomial modifier. We also tested models with observations truncated at 50, 75 and 100 m, as well as a model with observations grouped in intervals (5-8) between 0 and the maximum distance. To select among estimators, we chose the one which produced a detectability at or close to 1.0 for distance = 0 (Buckland et al. 2001).

Table 4. Number of point count sites by habitat, and years in which point count surveys were conducted, in different habitat types, for the landbird monitoring program at Channel Islands National Park.

Island	Habitat	1994	1995	1996	1997	1998	2000	2001	2002	2003	2004	2005	2006	2007	2008	2009
AN	Coreopsis scrub									5	5	5	4			4
AN	Grassland									1	1	2	1			
AN	Perennial iceplant									1	1					
SB	Boxthorn scrub							1	1	1	1	1		1	1	1
SB	Cactus scrub							1	2	2	1	1		1	1	1
SB	Coreopsis scrub							1	5	5	3	5		3	2	3
SB	Grassland							4	10	16	13	16		12	12	15
SB	Perennial iceplant								1	1	1	2		2	2	2
SB	Sea cliff scrub								1	1	1	1		1	1	1
SB	Seablite scrub									1		4		4	3	3
SM	Baccharis scrub								1	1	1	1	1	1	1	1
SM	Caliche scrub								2	2	2	2	2	2	2	2
SM	Coastal bluff scrub								1	1	1	1	1	1	1	1
SM	Coastal sage scrub								2	2	2	2	2	2	2	2
SM	Scrub (non-spec)								5	5	5	5	5	5	5	5
SM	Coreopsis scrub								8	8	8	8	8	7	8	8
SM	Grassland								11	11	11	11	11	10	11	11
SM	Lupine scrub								8	8	8	8	8	8	8	8
SM	Riparian herbaceous								1	1	1	1	1	1	1	1
SM	Riparian woodland									1	1	1	1	1	1	1
SR	Closed Cone Pine									6			6		5	6
SR	Coastal sage scrub								13	9			37		31	37
SR	Grassland								24	21			30		16	30
SR	Island chaparral			5	5	5	5	5	14	20			35		25	30
SR	Island Oak	9		7	6	7			8	11			13		3	6
SR	Lupine scrub												5		5	5
SR	Mixed woodland			9	10	10	10	12	13	18			21		17	9
SR	Riparian	20	20	16	16	14	20	20	20	26			28		28	8
SR	Riparian herbaceous									3		4			4	4
SR	Riparian woodland									3		4			4	4
SR	Torrey pine	10		8			10		15	16			16		16	6

11

For both transect and point count data, we estimated islandwide annual density for each species, pooled over transects and point count sites, respectively. Trends were assessed by regression of density versus year. We also used regression to compare islandwide density estimates for transects and point counts among species.

For species with an inadequate number of observations to construct detectability curves, it is possible to estimate density using detectability curves from other, similar species. The number of rock wren detections on line transects (36) was by itself inadequate to estimate density, so we constructed a detectability function for that species by pooling its line transect observations with those of Bewick's wrens. Rock wrens and Bewick's wrens had similar detection functions on point counts (Table 6).

Table 5. Number of detections on line transects (LT) and on point counts (PC) for breeding landbirds at Channel Islands National Park.

Common Name	LT	PC
Red-tailed hawk	26	81
Northern harrier	68	63
Peregrine falcon	23	25
American kestrel	86	88
California quail		82
Mourning dove		38
Barn owl	21	4
Short-eared owl	17	3
Burrowing owl	4	
White-throated swift		11
Anna's hummingbird	20	104
Allen's hummingbird	253	405
Pacific-slope flycatcher	3	671
Black phoebe	5	75
Horned lark	878	722
Barn swallow	27	146
Common raven	171	677
Rock wren	36	92
Bewick's wren	56	1231
Northern mockingbird	1	42
Loggerhead shrike		25
European starling	22	7
Hutton's vireo	1	13
Orange-crowned warbler	1659	1930
Rufous-crowned sparrow		2
Song sparrow	1971	2348
Spotted towhee	2	1234
Chipping sparrow	2	935
Western meadowlark	1426	1727
Lesser goldfinch	1	414
House finch	93	929

From 2001-2005 distances over 100 m for line transect sampling and over 50 m for point count sampling were not estimated, but were recorded as "> 100 m" and " > 50 m", respectively. A total of 1045 records (out of 22,463), involving 16 species was recorded in this manner. In most cases, this represented <5% of the distances recorded for each species (and which were used to construct detectability curves and density estimates). However, for 5 species (American kestrel, Bewick's wren, common raven, red-tailed hawk and western meadowlark) the number of records recorded in this manner on point counts (but not line transects) exceeded 10% of the total number of records later used to estimate detection and probability. For those data we considered 100 m and 50 m to be the respective distance to the bird. Truncated data in distance sampling can result in inflated density estimates and wider confidence intervals (Stanbury and Gregory 2009), and so point count density estimate for those 5 species may be over-estimated.

Table 6. Results of analysis with program Distance for both line transect and point count data. N = number of detections; PDF (SE) = value of probability density function at zero distance, with standard error; %CV = coefficient of variation for PDF; p = probability of detection; ESW = effective strip width, for line transects; ERD = effective radial distance, for point counts; T = truncated; I = intervals.

Species	N	PDF (SE)	%CV	p	ESW/ERD	Model	T/I
Line Transects							
Northern harrier*	68	0.0069 (0.0006)	9.2	0.301	144.6	Uniform	
American kestrel*	86	0.0131 (0.0012)	8.8	0.254	76.1	Hazard rate	
Allen's hummingbird*	253	0.0697 (0.0042)	6.1	0.143	14.3	Hazard rate	
Horned lark	878	0.0320 (0.0009)	2.9	0.312	31.3	Hazard rate	T 100
Common raven*	167	0.0132 (0.0009)	6.5	0.223	75.6	Half-normal	
Rock wren/Bewick's wren	88**	0.0256 (0.0021)	8.3	0.519	35.0	Hazard rate	T 75
Orange-crowned warbler	1659	0.0312 (0.0007)	2.9	0.267	32.0	Half-normal	
Song sparrow	1968	0.0305 (0.0006)	2.0	0.234	32.7	Half-normal	
Western meadowlark*	1426	0.0152 (0.0005)	3.4	0.330	66.7	Uniform	
House finch*	93	0.0274 (0.0016)	6.0	0.562	36.5	Uniform	
Point Counts							
Northern harrier	52	0.0007 (0.00014)	20.6	0.126	53.1	Hazard rate	I
American kestrel	90	0.0007 (0.00008)	10.7	0.051	51.9	Hazard rate	
California quail	81	0.0004 (0.00005)	11.9	0.029	67.5	Hazard rate	
Anna's hummingbird*	81	0.0069 (0.00095)	13.8	0.115	17.0	Half-normal	
Allen's hummingbird*	379	0.0096 (0.00049)	5.1	0.021	14.5	Half-normal	T 100
Pacific-slope flycatcher*	663	0.0020 (0.00007)	3.8	0.036	31.6	Half-normal	
Black phoebe	59	0.0031 (0.0010)	31.9	0.014	25.3	Half-normal	T 75
Horned lark	722	0.0011 (0.0001)	4.2	0.014	43.3	Hazard rate	
Barn swallow*	119	0.0013 (0.0001)	10.2	0.070	39.6	Half-normal	I
Common raven*	663	0.0003 (0.00003)	8.5	0.013	78.5	Hazard rate	
Rock wren	92	0.0005 (0.00006)	14.8	0.044	62.7	Hazard rate	
Bewick's wren	1168	0.0016 (0.00005)	3.0	0.057	35.9	Half-normal	
Orange-crowned warbler	1884	0.0012 (0.00003)	2.7	0.018	41.0	Half-normal	
Song sparrow*	2289	0.1226 (0.00004)	3.5	0.016	40.4	Hazard rate	
Spotted towhee	1214	0.0011 (0.00003)	2.9	0.015	42.7	Hazard rate	
Chipping sparrow	934	0.0011 (0.00006)	5.4	0.011	42.6	Half-normal	
Western meadowlark	1730	0.0005 (0.00001)	2.7	0.020	64.9	Hazard rate	
Lesser goldfinch	408	0.0018 (0.00059)	33.5	0.114	33.7	Half-normal	T 100
House finch*	852	0.0017 (0.00033)	18.2	0.111	33.3	Hazard rate	

*indicates model did not include observer as covariate
**Rock wren and Bewick's wren observations were combined to construct a detectability curve for rock wrens

For some species that did not have adequate detections to estimate density (i.e., European starling, Hutton's vireo, mourning dove and northern mockingbird), we present the total number of individuals observed annually on each island during surveys (including some fall surveys, which are not used to estimate density). We also present such numbers for red-tailed hawks, for which detectability could not be adequately modeled. Although trends are difficult to infer from raw count numbers, at the very least such data suggest relative abundance and presence or absence on that island.

Habitat Use and Selection

We evaluated habitat use and selection from point count data for the 15 resident species that had large enough sample sizes for meaningful analyses. We excluded raptors and the common raven from the analyses because they were generally observed in flight and could not be associated with a particular habitat type on any given count. The pooled results are weighted toward habitat use on Santa Rosa, because of the number of point count sites (145) on that island. Because of Santa Rosa's size relative to that of the other three islands included in this study, it contains >80% of habitat available to landbirds. Therefore we also evaluated habitat use separately for each island.

Habitat use was evaluated with diversity profiles (Tothmeresz 1995). Diversity profiles are constructed from the mathematical relationship between different alpha diversity measures (Renyi 1961, Hill 1973) and allow an evaluation across scale parameters (α) for different diversity indices. The scale parameters have decreasing sensitivity to low abundance objects (species and habitat categories) and can range from 0 to infinity. Diversity among objects is evaluated by the levels and slopes of the profiles; profiles of objects that do not cross can unambiguously be said to differ in diversity, but when profiles cross then interpretation of diversity must be made in the context of different levels of α. We constructed two sets of profiles; the first set evaluated bird diversity in the nine general habitat classes and the second evaluated how diverse habitat use was for each of the 15 bird species. The habitat classes included bare ground, chaparral, coastal bluff, grassland, iceplant, pine forest, riparian, scrub, and woodland. The profiles were developed from data pooled across the islands.

Habitat selection was analyzed with a two-step process. The first step consisted of conducting log-likelihood χ^2 tests (χ^2_{ll}) to determine if there was an overall pattern of habitat selection for each species. If the χ^2_{ll} test for a species was significant ($p > 0.05$) we then conducted χ^2_{ll} tests and constructed 95% confidence intervals to test proportional occurrence (o_i) versus proportional availability (π_i) in each of the nine habitat classes (Manly Design 1; Manly et al. 2002). We calculated proportional occurrence as the number of observations of a species within each habitat class (i) divided by the total number of observations for that species. Availability was calculated as the number of point count stations within each habitat class divided by the total number of stations. Significance of the χ^2_{ll} value within each habitat class was evaluated by comparing it to a Bonferroni-adjusted critical χ^2_{ll} value. Unstandardized habitat selection ratios ($\hat{w}_i$) were calculated as o_i/π_i and standardized selection ratios (B$_i$) as $\hat{w}_i/\Sigma\hat{w}_i$ (Manly et al. 2002). Two groups of analyses were conducted; use by island and use pooled across islands. Data were pooled across years because of low annual sample sizes for most species.

Analyses were conducted with the Adehabitat and BiodiversityR packages in R (R Development Core Team; http://www.R-project.org).

14

15

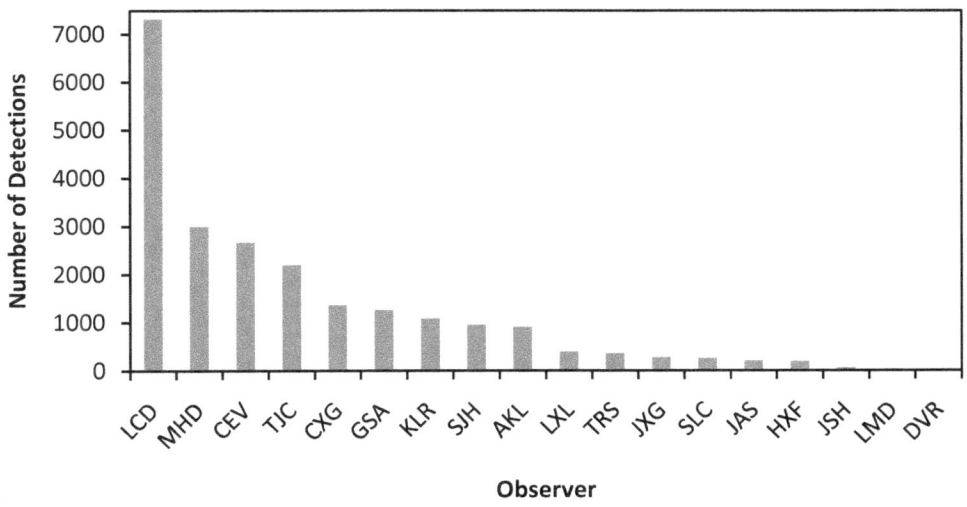

Figure 6. Number of detections per observer for landbird monitoring at Channel Islands National Park, 1993-2009.

Results

Due to the vagaries of staffing, a total of 20 observers collected data over the 17 years of sampling, with number of detections ranging from 16-7,320 per observer (Fig. 6). A total of 113 species were observed across al islands, including 33 of the 35 species that breed on San Miguel, Santa Rosa, Anacapa and Santa Barbara Islands (Table 4). A total of 21 of those species had sufficient detections on either line transects or point counts to estimate density (Table 6). Species that did not have sufficient detections included those which, in the park, breed only on Santa Cruz Island. Great blue herons, which breed only in one location on Santa Rosa Island (Jaw Gulch; D. Richards, NPS, unpubl. data), also generally were not recorded on surveys, nor were bald eagles, which began breeding on Santa Cruz in 2006, nor golden eagles, which bred at two sites on Santa Rosa Island from 1997-2005 (Collins and Latta 2006). Loggerhead shrikes are known to be rare, and were not observed in sufficient abundance for density estimation on Santa Rosa point counts. Other species thought to be more common but which were not recorded in sufficient abundance included mourning doves, rock wrens, northern mockingbirds, Hutton's vireos, and rufous-crowned sparrows (which breed on Santa Cruz and West Anacapa Island, neither of which was surveyed in this effort). Swifts and swallows were rarely observed. Additionally, barn swallows are thought to be summer residents (Jones et al. 1999), and may not have arrived on the islands in large numbers by the time monitoring was conducted in the spring. Nocturnal birds, such as the owl species, were not observed in appreciable numbers on transects or point counts.

The density estimators chosen differed among species (Table 6). The coefficient of variation for the probability detection function (PDF) was similar for both methods, although generally lower for line transect data. The coefficient of variation for PDF was high (>20%) for northern harriers, black phoebes, and lesser goldfinches on point counts. For those species detected in sufficient numbers with both methods, the probability of detection was up to 10 times greater on line transects, though the effective strip width distances were similar to the effective radial distances. Effective strip width and effective radial distances were greater for large, conspicuous species such as raptors and common ravens, and for western meadowlarks (perhaps due to their loud song), and low for Allen's and Anna's hummingbirds.

Examination of detection probability plots showed few problems with fitted models (see Appendix A, Detection Probability Plots). Several species did not show a classic curve of attenuation, in which detection falls off with increasing distance from the transect midline or point-count center. Bewick's wrens were observed more at 30 m than at distance = 0 on line transects. American kestrels were observed more frequently at 50 m on point counts, while western meadowlarks were observed more often at 30-50 m than at lesser distances, on both line transects and point counts. On line transects, Bewick's wrens may have been observed less close to the transect midline because they are small in size and may have flushed from locations close to the transect midline and then were observed at greater distances. Western meadowlarks are large and sing conspicuously, so it is unclear why they would have been observed less at distances close to the transect midline. On point counts, they may have been flushed from locations near the center point as observers approached, and before data was recorded. Meadowlarks typically occur in low, open grassland habitats, in which birds flushing from near point-count locations may be more of a problem than in other habitat types.

Trends for Individual Species

Northern Harrier

Northern harriers increased on San Miguel transects over time (Fig. 7a; $r^2 = 57.8$, $F = 20.137$, $p = 0.0006$), occurring at or near zero density from 1993 through 1996. Harriers fluctuated on Santa Barbara transects, but did not increase ($F = 1.075$, $p = 0.3242$). Northern harriers were not observed on Santa Rosa point counts until 2006 (Fig. 7b). They fluctuated on Santa Barbara point counts, and peaked and then declined on San Miguel point counts.

a)   b)

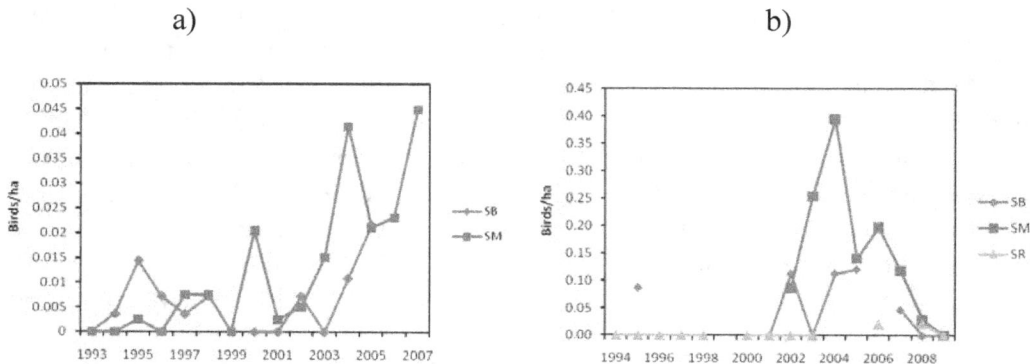

Figure 7. Islandwide densities of northern harriers estimated from line transects (a) and point counts (b), 1993-2009 (SB = Santa Barbara Island, SM = San Miguel Island, SR = Santa Rosa Island).

American Kestrel

American kestrels fluctuated on Santa Barbara Island but disappeared from San Miguel (Figs. 8a and 8b) and declined on Santa Rosa (Fig 5b; $r^2 = 83.6$, $F = 51.880$, $p < 0.0001$). No American kestrels were observed on San Miguel from 2004-2008, and none were observed on Santa Rosa in 2008.

a)   b)

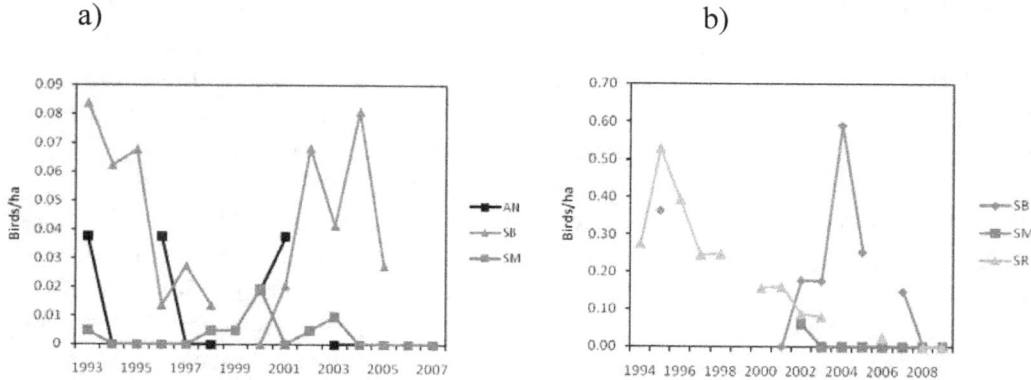

Figure 8. Islandwide densities of American kestrels estimated from line transects (a) and point counts (b), 1993-2009 (AN = Anacapa Island, SB = Santa Barbara Island, SM = San Miguel Island, SR = Santa Rosa Island).

California Quail

California quail, which occur only on Santa Rosa Island in the park, occurred at overall low densities on the island (1-4 per km^2, Fig. 9a), and declined over the study period ($r^2 = 47.2$, F = 9.939, p = 0.0116).

a)   b)

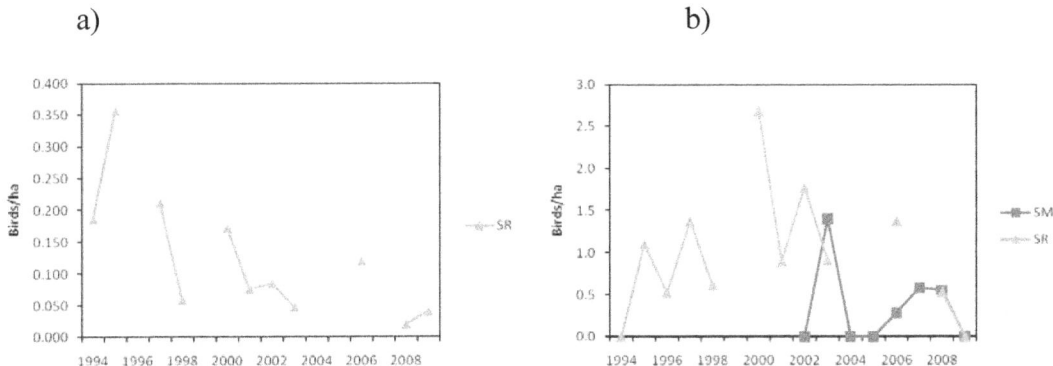

Figure 9. Islandwide densities of California quail (a) and Anna's hummingbird (b) estimated from point counts, 1994-2009 (SM = San Miguel Island, SR = Santa Rosa Island).

Anna's and Allen's Hummingbird

Anna's hummingbirds showed an increasing trend, with annual fluctuations, on Santa Rosa point counts prior to 2001 (Fig. 9b). No Anna's hummingbirds were recorded on either island in 2009. Allen's hummingbirds exhibited multi-year cycles on San Miguel transects (Fig. 10a) with the amplitude greatly increasing after island foxes (*Urocyon littoralis*) were brought into captivity in 1999. The amplitude is not nearly as pronounced in the point count data from San Miguel (Fig. 10b). Santa Rosa point count data showed Allen's hummingbirds increasing in the latter years of the fox decline (1999-2000) but then declining after 2001.

a)   b)

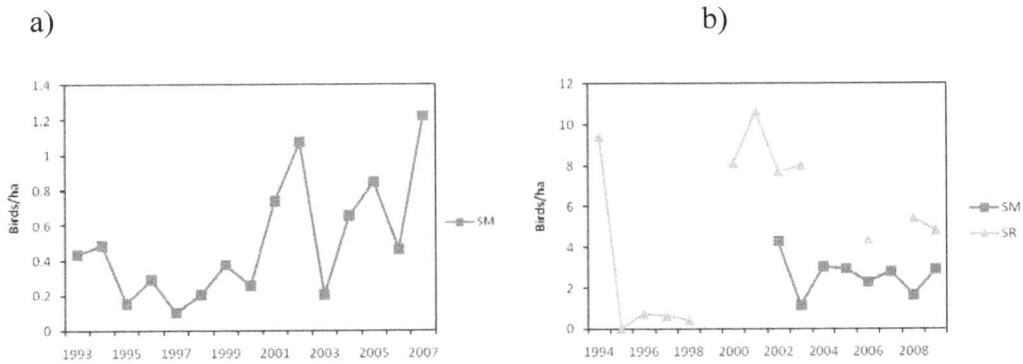

Figure 10. Islandwide densities of Allen's hummingbirds estimated from transects (a) and point counts (b), 1993-2009 (SB = Santa Barbara Island, SM = San Miguel Island, SR = Santa Rosa Island).

Pacific-slope Flycatcher and Black Phoebe

Both flycatcher species exhibited higher densities, with fluctuations, in the early part of the study period (Figs. 11a and 11b). However, prior to 2000, most points sampled were in riparian habitat (Table 3). Inclusion of points in other habitat types may have decreased overall density estimates. Pacific-slope flycatchers did not decline in riparian areas, but black phoebes did ($r^2 = 34.8$, F = 5.818, p = 0.0423). No black phoebes were observed on riparian point counts in 2008 or 2009 (NPS, unpubl. data). Only 3 were observed in 2008, 2 in coastal sage scrub and 1 in grasslands.

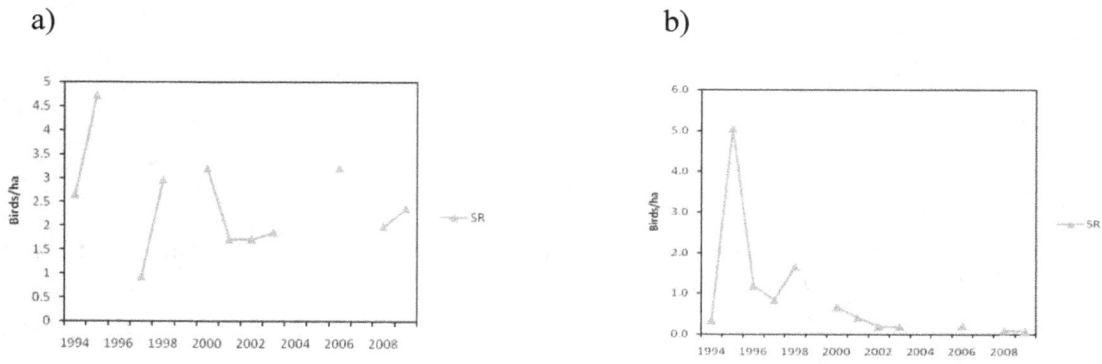

Figure 11. Islandwide densities of Pacific-slope flycatchers (a) and black phoebes (b) estimated from point counts, 1994-2009 (SR = Santa Rosa Island).

Horned Lark

Data from transects showed horned larks to be in a multi-year population cycle on Santa Barbara and San Miguel Islands (Fig. 12a). Densities from point counts also suggested higher densities and greater fluctuation on Santa Barbara, and showed larks to exist at low densities on Santa Rosa (Fig. 12b). No horned larks were recorded on Anacapa Island line transects or point counts.

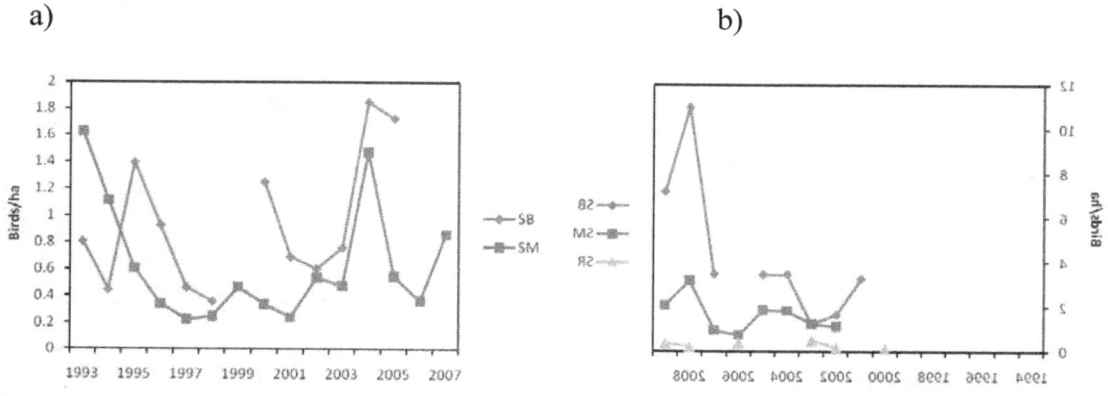

Figure 12. Islandwide densities of horned larks estimated from line transects (a) and point counts (b), 1993-2009 (SB = Santa Barbara Island, SM = San Miguel Island, SR = Santa Rosa Island).

Barn Swallow

The number of barn swallow observations on line transects (27) was not sufficient to estimate density. Density estimates from point counts showed barn swallows to exist at relatively higher densities on Santa Rosa, with considerable interannual variability (Fig. 13).

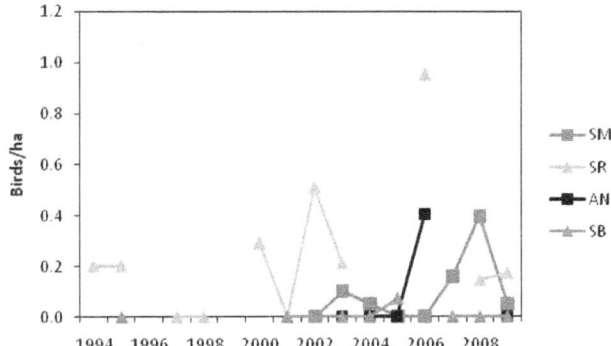

Figure 13. Islandwide densities of barn swallows estimated from point counts, 1994-2009 (AN = Anacapa Island, SB = Santa Barbara Island, SM = San Miguel Island, SR = Santa Rosa Island).

Common Raven

Density of common ravens on San Miguel line transects remained low from 1993-1997, then increased by a factor of 10 (Fig. 14a). Point count data also recorded the increase on Miguel, with a sharp decline from 2008 to 2009, and showed Santa Rosa raven densities to be lower than those on San Miguel (Fig. 14b). Densities on Santa Rosa increased over time (r^2 = 87.4, F = 77.284, p < 0.00001).

a)   b)

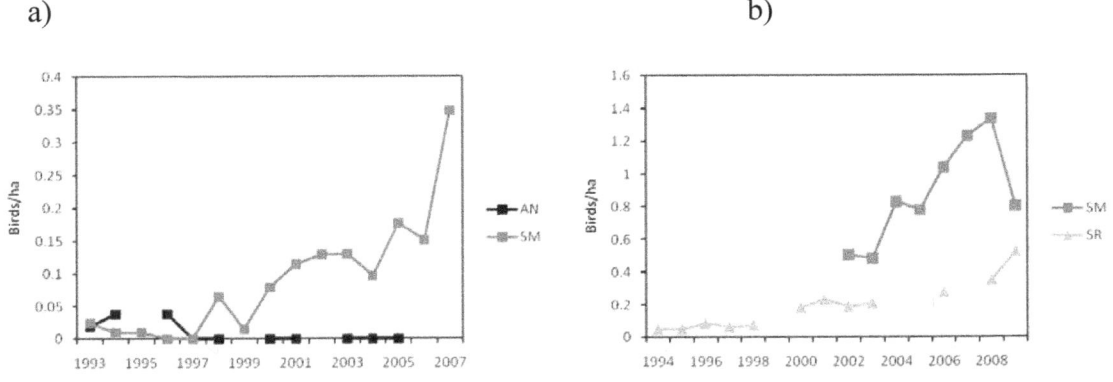

Figure 14. Islandwide densities of common ravens estimated from line transects (a) and point counts (b), 1993-2009 (AN = Anacapa Island, SM = San Miguel Island, SR = Santa Rosa Island).

21

Rock Wren and Bewick's Wren

Bewick's wrens were only observed consistently on Anacapa line transects, where density increased over time (Fig 15a; $r^2 = 82.9$, F = 44.868, p = 0.0002). Bewick's wrens remained fairly stable on Santa Rosa points counts, with some interannual variability, and fluctuated on Anacapa point counts from 2003-2009 (Fig. 15b). Rock wrens were observed inconsistently on Anacapa transects, fluctuated in a multi-year cycle on Santa Barbara, and disappeared from transects on San Miguel (Fig. 15c), where they were not observed after 2001. This decline was also reflected in point count densities (Fig. 15d); no rock wrens were observed on San Miguel point counts in 2005, 2006 or 2009. Rock wren density fluctuated markedly on Santa Rosa Island. Overall, rock wrens occurred at fairly low densities.

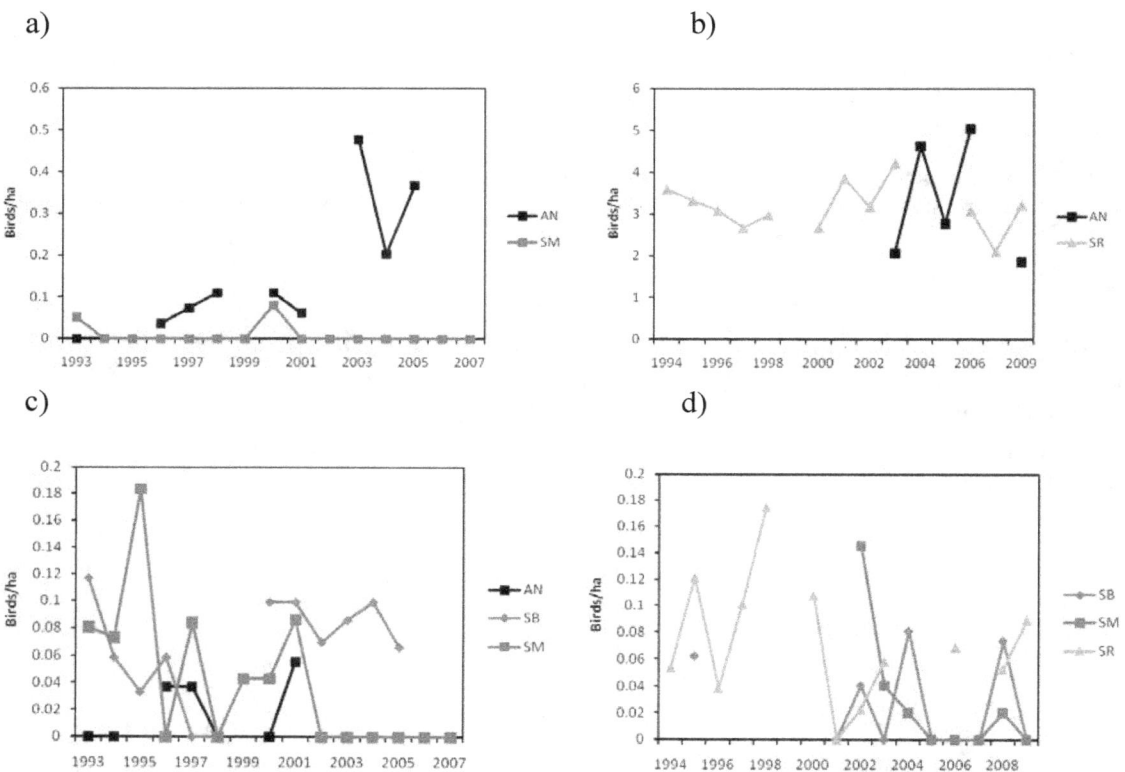

Figure 15. Islandwide densities of Bewick's wrens estimated from line transects (a) and point counts (b), and densities of rock wrens estimated from line transects (c) and point counts (d), 1993-2009 (AN = Anacapa Island, SB = Santa Barbara Island, SM = San Miguel Island, SR = Santa Rosa

Orange-crowned Warbler

Transect data showed orange-crowned warbler density to fluctuate in a similar fashion across the three islands (Fig. 16a). Orange-crowned warbler density on San Miguel transects increased over time, with the increase occurring after 1998 ($r^2 = 74.5$, F = 41.796, p < 0.0001). On Santa Barbara and Anacapa transects, orange-crowned warblers increased from 1998-2001 and then declined, with Anacapa showing another spike in 2005. Point count data showed orange-crowned warblers to fluctuate at lower levels on Santa Rosa and Santa Barbara, with no increase over time (Fig. 16b). The orange-crowned warbler increase on San Miguel and Anacapa after 2001 was reflected in the point count data, as well as in the transect data.

a)   b)

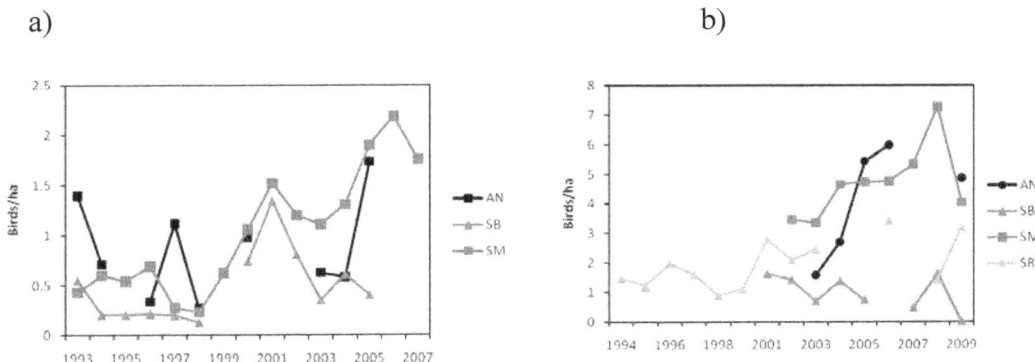

Figure 16. Islandwide densities of orange-crowned warblers estimated from transects (a) and point counts (b), 1993-2009 (AN = Anacapa Island, SB = Santa Barbara Island, SM = San Miguel Island, SR = Santa Rosa Island).

Song Sparrow

Song sparrow density on San Miguel transects steadily declined until 1998, after which it increased, but with considerable multi-year cycling (Fig 17a). This cycling was somewhat evident in point count data as well (Fig. 17b). Densities from point counts showed that Santa Rosa song sparrows exhibited multi-year cycling, with lower amplitude than on San Miguel. Song sparrow density on San Miguel was 4-5X that on Santa Rosa

a)   b)

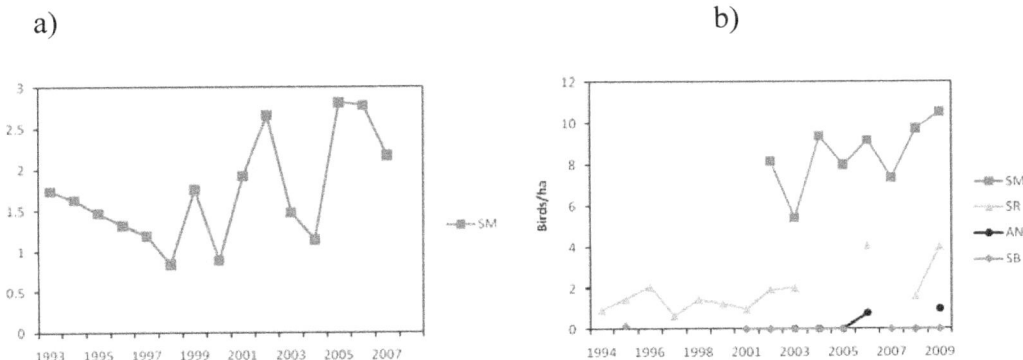

Figure 17. Islandwide densities of song sparrows estimated from line transects (a) and point counts (b), 1993-2009 (AN = Anacapa Island, SB = Santa Barbara Island, SM = San Miguel Island, SR = Santa Rosa Island).

Spotted Towhee and Chipping Sparrow

Density of spotted towhees on Santa Rosa Island fluctuated somewhat and increased over the study period (Fig. 18a), ($r^2 = 57.8$, F = 16.078, p = 0.0025). At densities of 1-3.5 birds/ha, spotted towhees were the most abundant of any species on Santa Rosa Island. Chipping sparrows decreased initially on Santa Rosa Island and then showed an increase, with some interannual fluctuation (Fig. 18b).

a)   b)

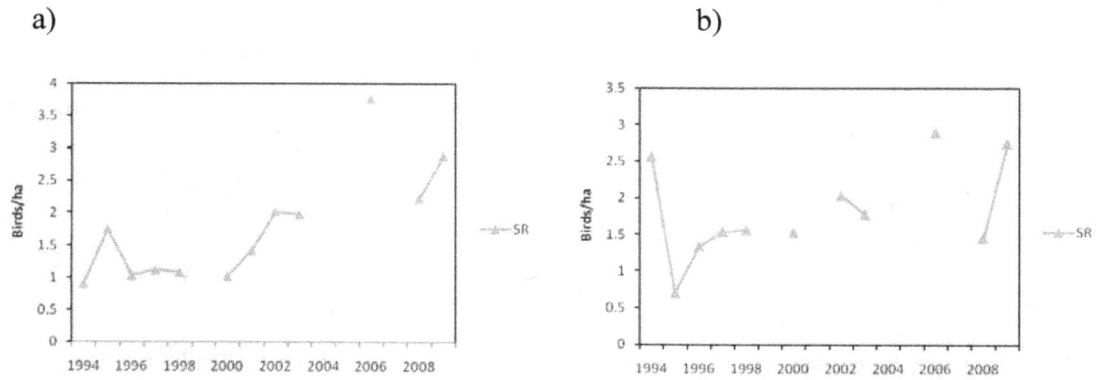

Figure 18. Islandwide densities of spotted towhees (a) and chipping sparrows (b) estimated from point counts, 1994-2009 (SR = Santa Rosa Island).

Western Meadowlark

Trends for western meadowlarks differed between transects and point counts. On the former, meadowlark density displayed multiyear cycles, with no apparent increase or decrease over time (Fig. 19a). Meadowlarks occurred at higher densities on Santa Barbara Island. Point count data, however (Fig. 19b), showed meadowlark density to decline on both Santa Barbara Island ($r^2 = 92.6$, F = 88.838, p < 0.0001) and increase on Santa Rosa Island ($r^2 = 62.9$, F = 19.712, p < 0.0001). San Miguel meadowlarks appeared to decline over much of the period, though the apparent decline was not statistically significant (F = 0.152, p = 0.710), likely due to the high value in 2009. As in the transect data, meadowlark densities were higher on Santa Barbara Island than on the other islands in the beginning of the period, but were similar at the end.

a)   b)

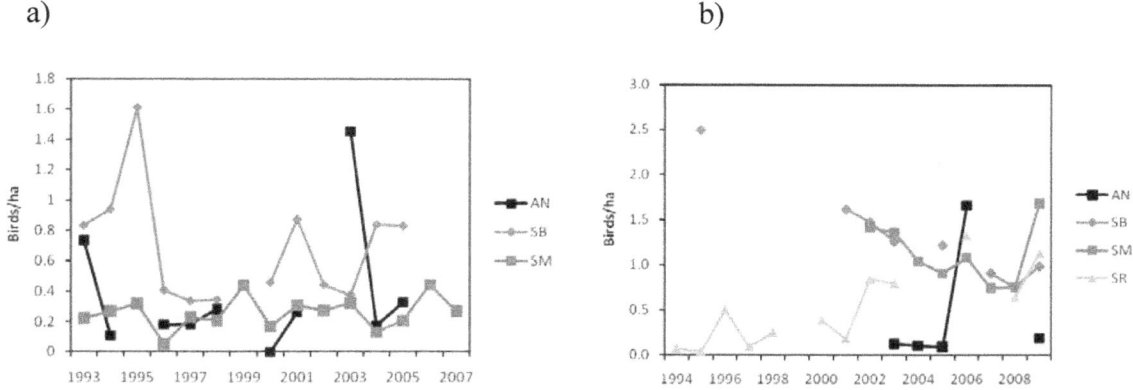

Figure 19. Islandwide densities of western meadowlarks estimated from transects (a) and point counts (b), 1994-2009 (AN = Anacapa Island, SB = Santa Barbara Island, SM = San Miguel Island, SR = Santa Rosa Island).

Lesser Goldfinch

The density of lesser goldfinches on Santa Rosa Island was variable, with generally higher density values occurring after 2001 (Fig. 20). Densities appeared to increase initially after 2001, peak in 2006, and decrease after that.

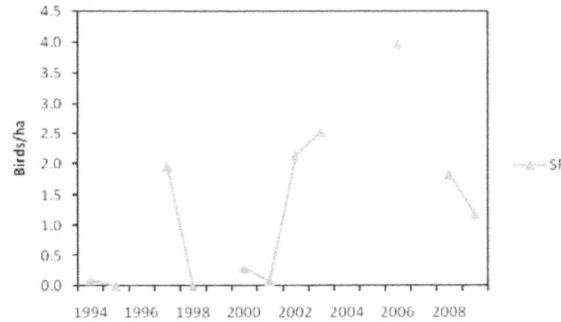

Figure 20. Islandwide densities of lesser goldfinches estimated from point counts, 1994-2009 (SR = Santa Rosa Island).

House Finch

House finches were only observed during two of the survey years on Santa Barbara transects. House finch density on Anacapa Island transects varied, and density on San Miguel transects declined over time (Fig. 21a, $r^2 = 60.1$, F = 22.738, p = 0.0004). No house finches were recorded on San Miguel in 2003 or 2005. House finches appeared to be most abundant on Santa Rosa Island in 1995-1996, but this may reflect the fact that primarily riparian point count sites were sampled prior to 2001 on Santa Rosa.

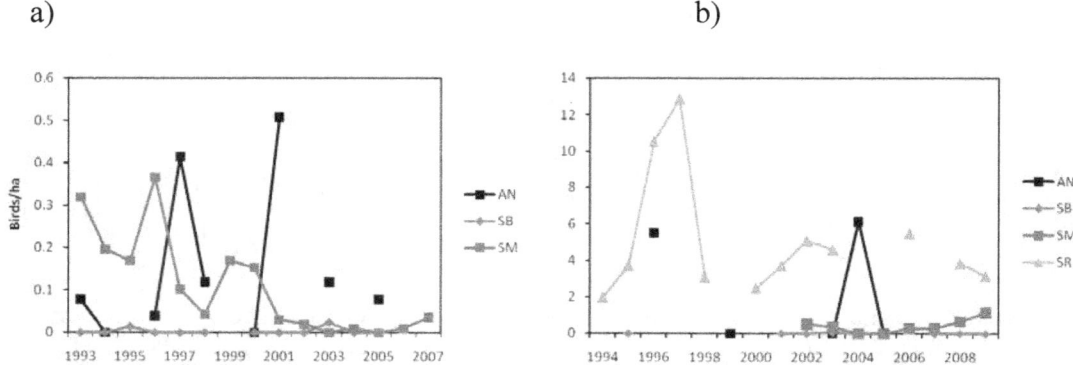

a)   b)

Figure 21. Islandwide densities of house finches estimated from line transects (a) and point counts (b), 1993-2009 (AN = Anacapa Island, SB = Santa Barbara Island, SM = San Miguel Island, SR = Santa Rosa Island).

Comparison of Densities from Line Transects and Point Counts

For 9 species, we were able to compare annual island-wide densities from line transects with those from point counts (Table 7, Appendix B). None of these data are from Santa Rosa, since line transect sampling was not conducted on that island. For 5 of the 9 species, point count densities were correlated with line transect densities. Of those for which the regression was not significant, sample size (<6) was low and additional data may have resulted in a stronger association. House finches were the one species for which the data suggested no relationship at all between point count and line transect densities. House finches occur in specific habitat types and/or geographic areas, and island-wide densities may not reflect specific densities in those habitats.

Point count densities were higher than those from line transect densities for all species except the raptors. For the northern harrier, point count densities approximated those from line transects (regression slope close to 1.0) while for the American kestrel point count densities were less than those from line transects (regression slope <1.0).

Table 7. Regression of islandwide annual densities from point counts on annual densities from line transects. Slope of regression line (β) is shown for those regressions that were significant.

Species	n	r^2	F	p	β
Northern harrier	9	63.7	15.049	0.006	0.90
American kestrel	6	47.1	5.446	0.080	
Allen's hummingbird	6	50.6	6.136	0.068	
Horned lark	11	44.7	9.086	0.015	1.93
Common raven	6	38.5	4.128	0.120	
Orange-crowned warbler	17	72.8	43.833	<0.001	2.90
Song sparrow	5	84.8	23.350	0.017	3.17
Western meadowlark	13	52.2	14.084	0.003	1.88
House finch	7	-12.1	0.015	0.578	

Habitat Use and Selection Pooled Across Islands

The habitat types used least by the 15 bird species included bare ground, iceplant, and coastal bluff; the diversity profiles for these three types were lower than those of the other six types for all levels of Renyi's alpha (Figure 22). The number of species occurring in chaparral, coastal scrub, grassland, pine forest, riparian, and woodland were similar (Renyi's alpha levels < 0.5; Figure 22), but use of chaparral, pine forest, riparian, and woodland was greater than grasslands and coastal scrub as alpha levels increased (Renyi's alpha $\geq$ 0.5; Figure 22). With the exception of grasslands, avian use of shrub and tree habitats was greater than use of habitats dominated by low herbaceous cover or bare ground (Table 8).

Table 8. The number of avian species (N = 15) in each of nine habitat types, from 1993 through 2008.

Habitat	Species
Bare	3
Bluff	5
Chaparral	15
Grassland	15
Iceplant	5
Pine	15
Riparian	15
Scrub	15
Woodland	15

The diversity profiles for the 15 species were indicative of complex patterns of habitat use (Figure 23). All of the species occurred in at least five habitat types (Table 9), but patterns of their relative abundance among the types differed considerably (Figure 23). Chipping sparrows, spotted towhees, lesser goldfinches, and house finches generally had the most equitable relative abundance patterns among the habitat types they occurred in, while those of black phoebes, song sparrows, rock wrens, and horned larks were much greater in certain habitats than in others (Figure 23).

The χ^2_{11} tests of general patterns of habitat selection were significant for all sixteen species ($P < 0.0001$). Profiles of unstandardized habitat selection ratios ($\hat{w}_i$) for each species are given in Figure 24 and standardized selection ratios (B_i) are presented in Appendix C. Allen's and Anna's hummingbirds, Bewick's wren, chipping sparrow, house finch, lesser goldfinch, Pacific-slope flycatcher, orange-crowned warbler, and spotted towhee generally showed strongest selection for chaparral, pine forest, riparian, and/or woodland habitats. Horned lark, song sparrow, white-crowned sparrow, and Western meadowlark generally showed selection for grassland and/or coastal scrub habitats. Black phoebe and rock wren appeared to be the most specialized, with strong selection for riparian habitat.

Habitat Selection by Island

With the exception of house finches on San Miguel Island and Allen's hummingbird, Anna's hummingbird and California quail on Santa Rosa Island, χ^2_{II} tests of general patterns of habitat selection were significant for all species/island combinations ($P < 0.0100$). Standardized selection ratios (B_i) are presented in Appendix D and profiles of unstandardized habitat selection ratios ($\hat{w}_i$) for each species are given in Appendix E. In some cases, species that occurred on islands with different habitat types had varying habitat selection patterns. For example, Bewick's wren selected coastal scrub habitat on Anacapa but tended to avoid that type on Santa Rosa. Other species, such as horned larks, showed consistent selection patterns across islands (Appendix D and E). The distribution patterns of the standardized selection ratios indicated that there was a greater tendency by species to avoid rather than select particular habitats (Appendix D and E); the magnitude of the standardized selection ratios tended to decrease as the number of habitats on the islands increased (Figure 25).

Table 9. The number of habitat types (N = 9) used by avian species from 1993 through 2008.

Species	Habitat Types
Allen's hummingbird	6
Anna's humingbird	6
Bewick's wren	7
Black phoebe	6
California quail	6
Chipping sparrow	6
House finch	6
Horned lark	9
Lesser goldfinch	6
Orange-crowned warbler	7
Pacific-slope flycatcher	6
Rock wren	5
Song sparrow	5
Spotted towhee	6
Western meadowlark	9

That is, on larger islands with a greater number of habitats, selection for habitats was weaker overall. On Santa Rosa, none of the selection ratios were > 0.4, and most were ≤ 0.2; all other islands had some selection ratios in the 0.6-1.0 range.

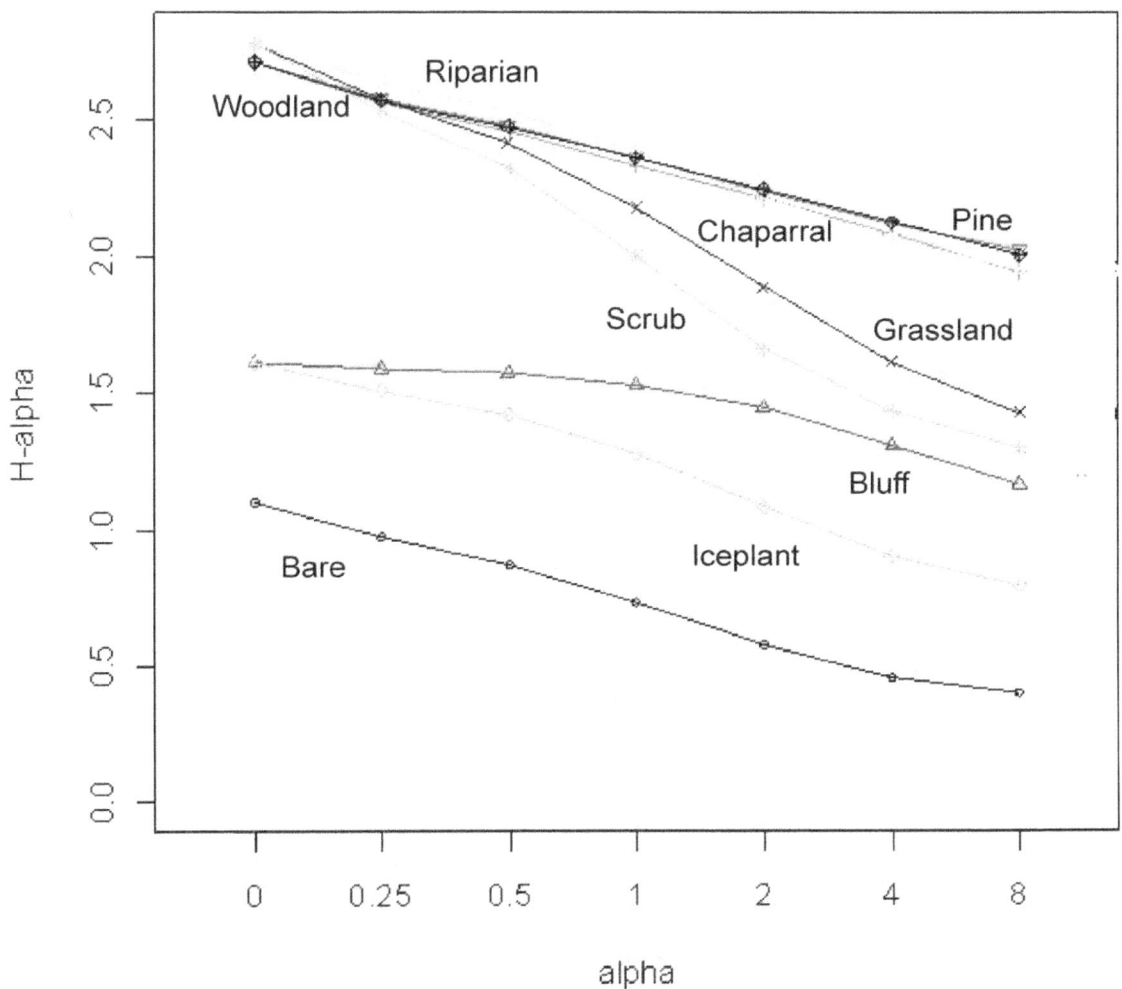

Figure 22. Diversity profiles of avian use (N = 16 species) in nine habitat types on Anacapa, Santa Barbara, San Miguel, and Santa Rosa Islands from 1993 through 2008. The parameter alpha is based on Renyi's (1961) scale of diversity. At alpha = 0, habitats with equivalent species richness (number of species) have equivalent diversity. Increasing alpha levels take abundance into account, so habitats with equitable number of individuals of multiple species have equivalent diversity levels; those with greater abundance of common species have lower diversity levels.

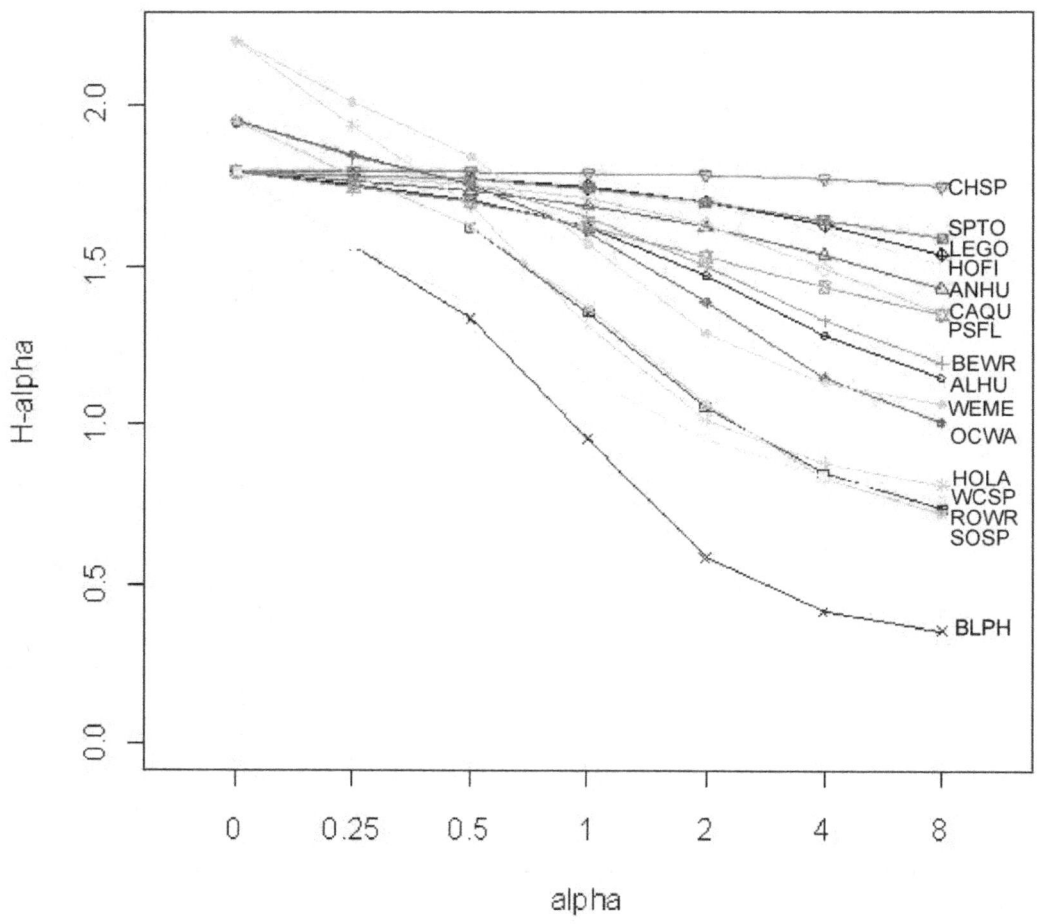

Figure 23. Diversity profiles of habitat use (N = 9 habitat types; see Figure 1) by 15 bird species on Anacapa, Santa Barbara, San Miguel, and Santa Rosa Islands from 1993 through 2008. The parameter alpha is based on Renyi's (1961) scale of diversity.

Figure 24. Unstandardized habitat selection ratio profiles, with 95% confidence intervals, for 15 species. Ratios above 1.0 denote selection for a habitat type; those below 1.0 denote avoidance.

California Quail

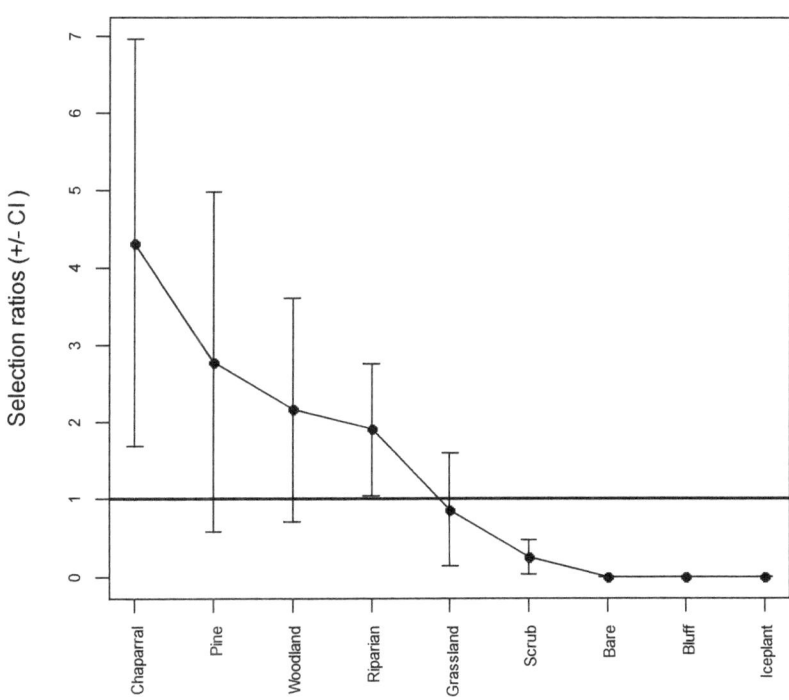

Anna's Hummingbird

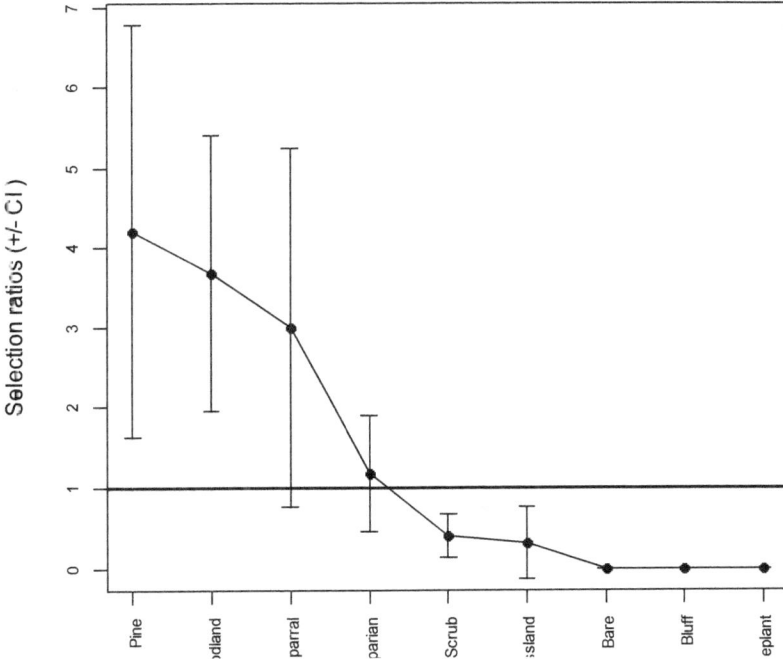

Figure 24, cont.

Allen's Hummingbird

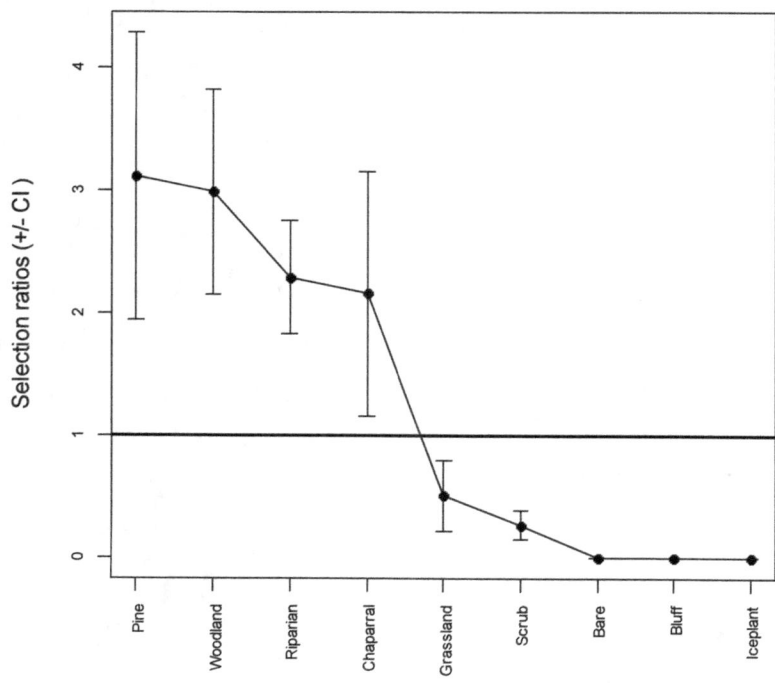

Pacific-slope Flycatcher

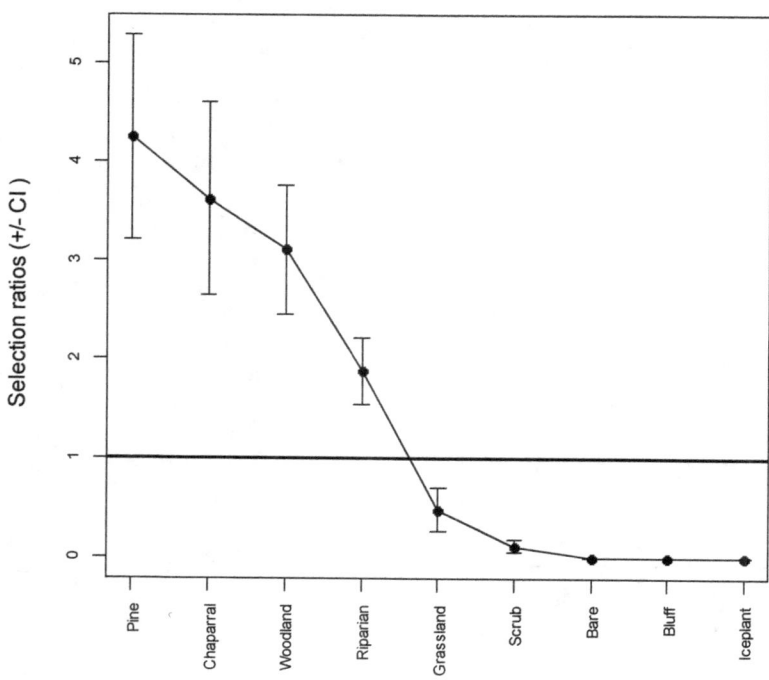

Figure 24, cont.

Black Phoebe

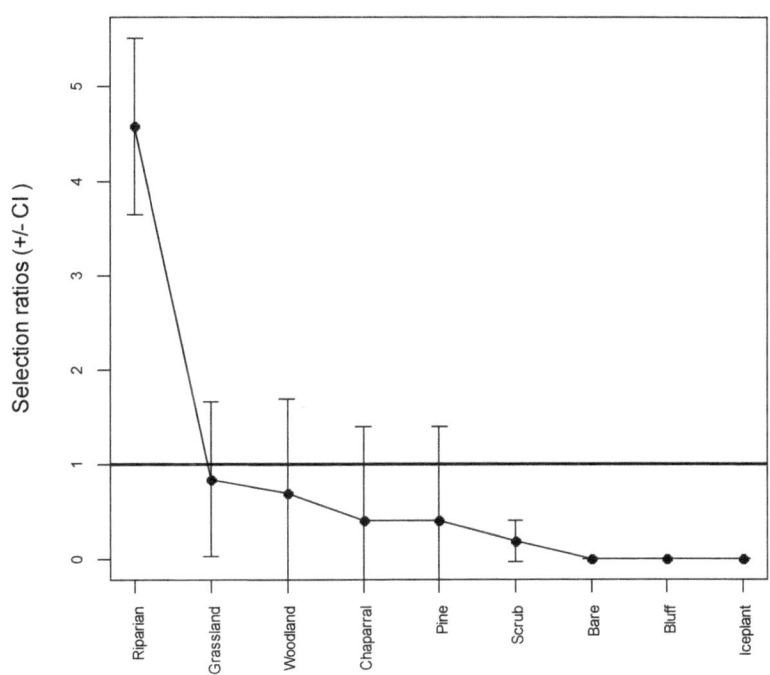

Horned Lark

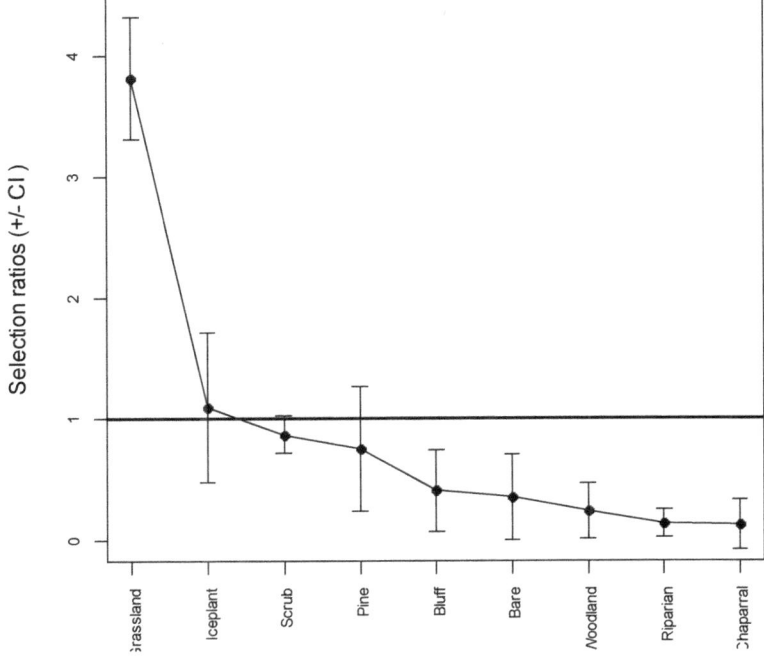

Figure 24, cont.

Rock Wren

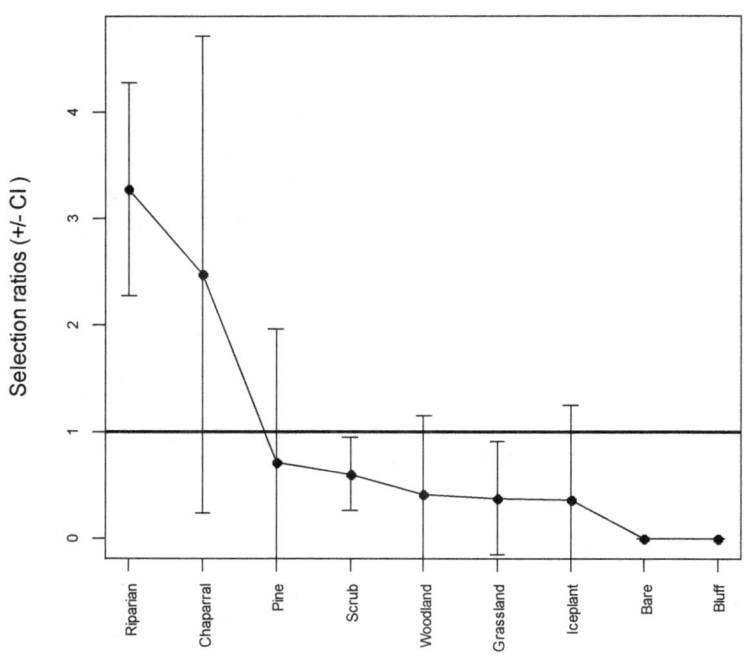

Bewick's Wren

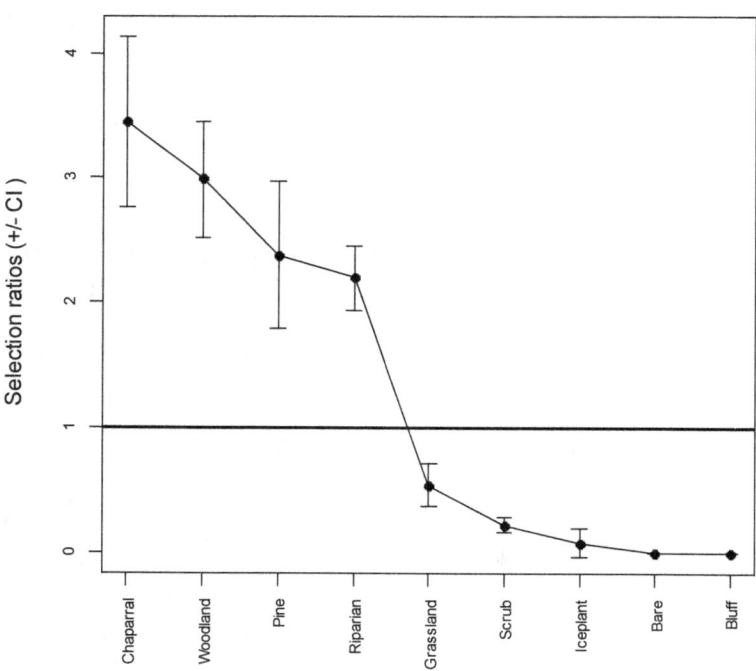

Figure 24, cont.

Orange-crowned Warbler

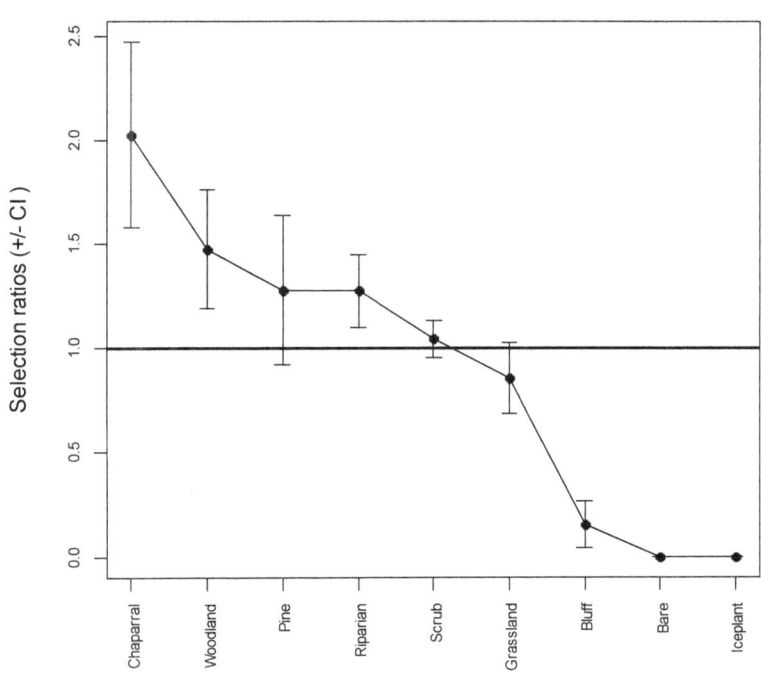

Song Sparrow

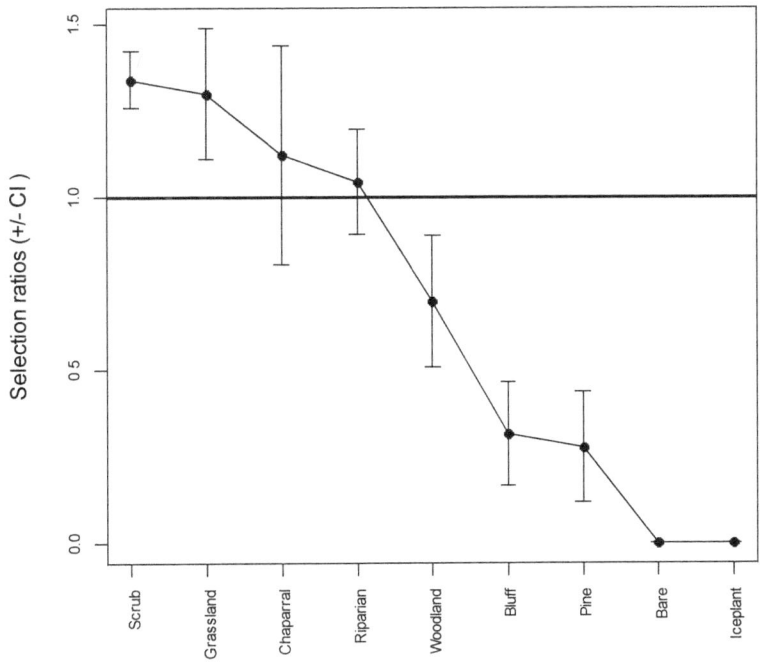

Figure 24, cont.

Spotted Towhee

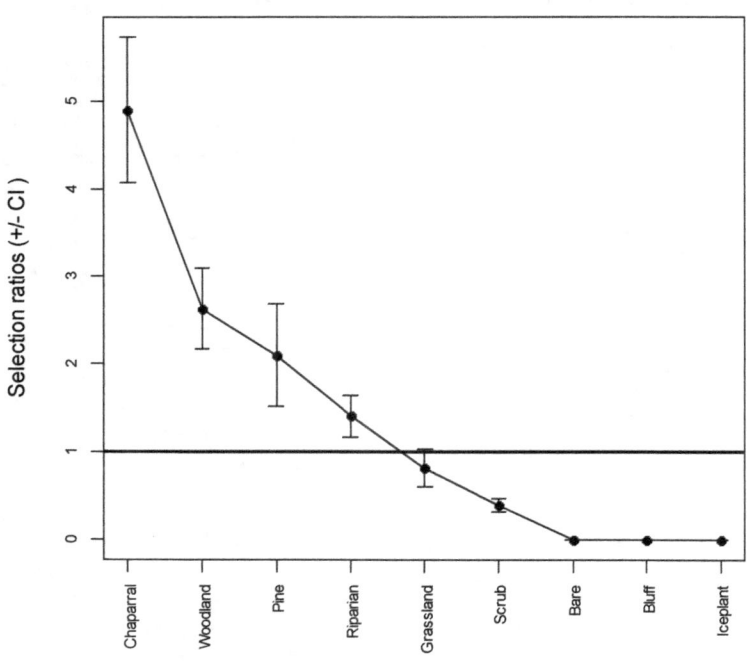

Chipping Sparrow

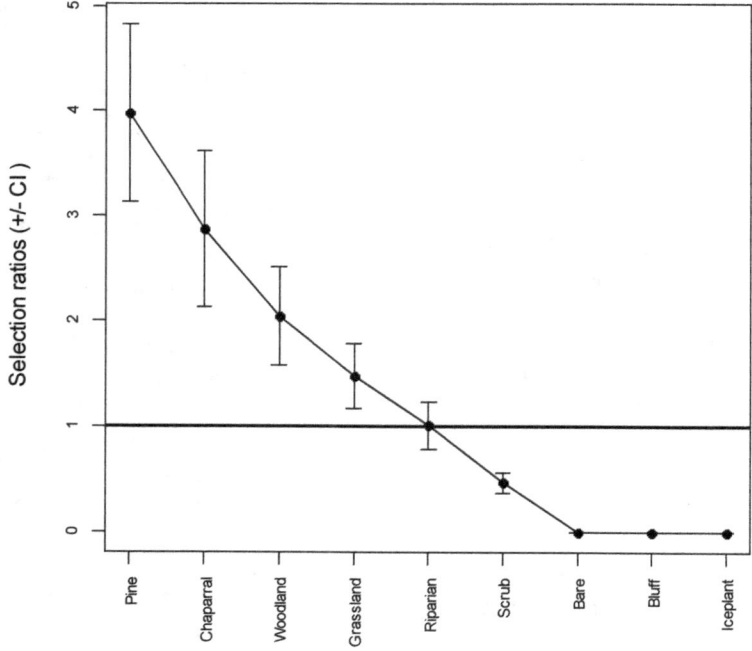

Western Meadowlark

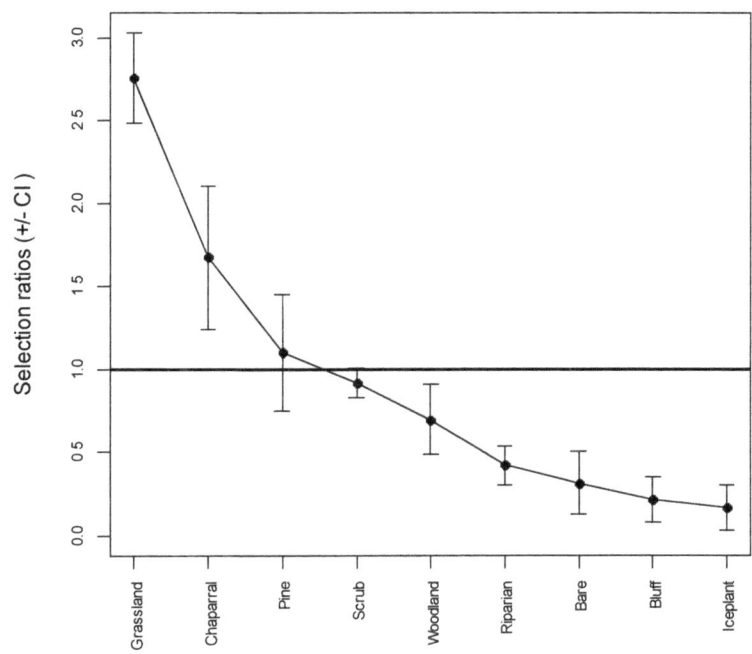

Lesser Goldfinch

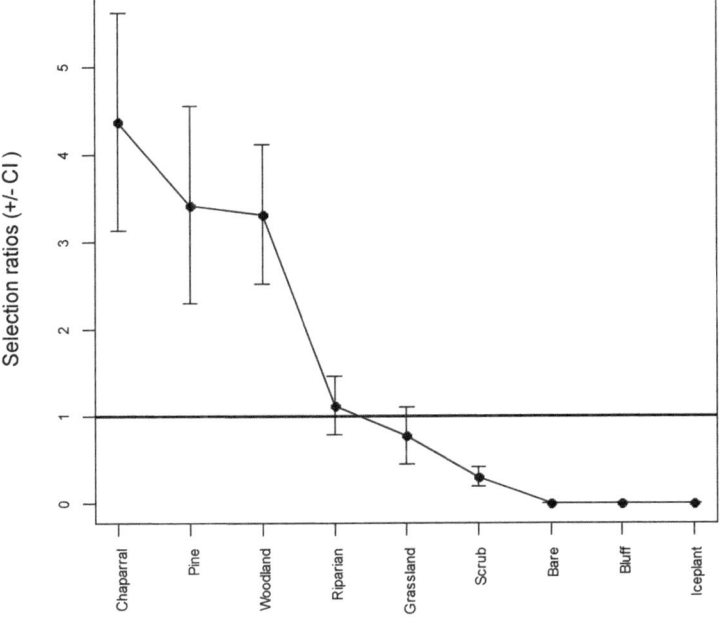

Figure 24, cont.

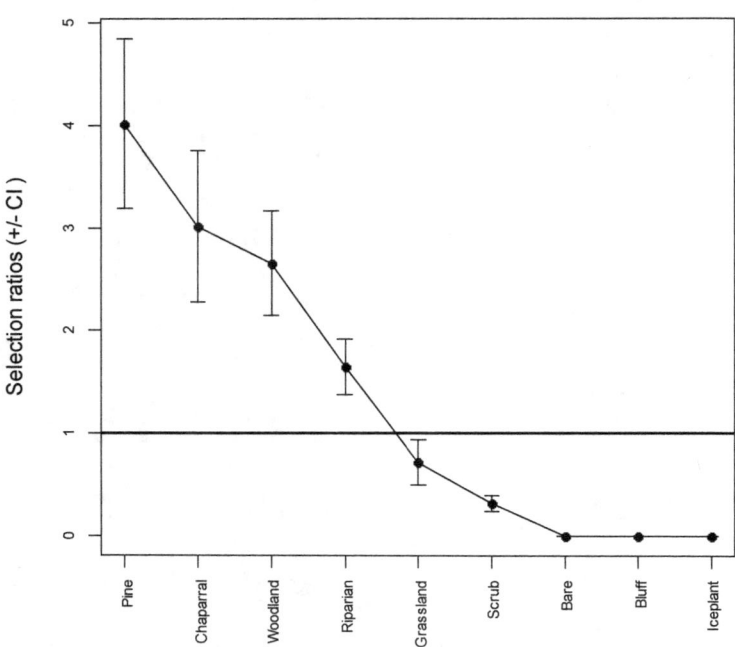

House Finch

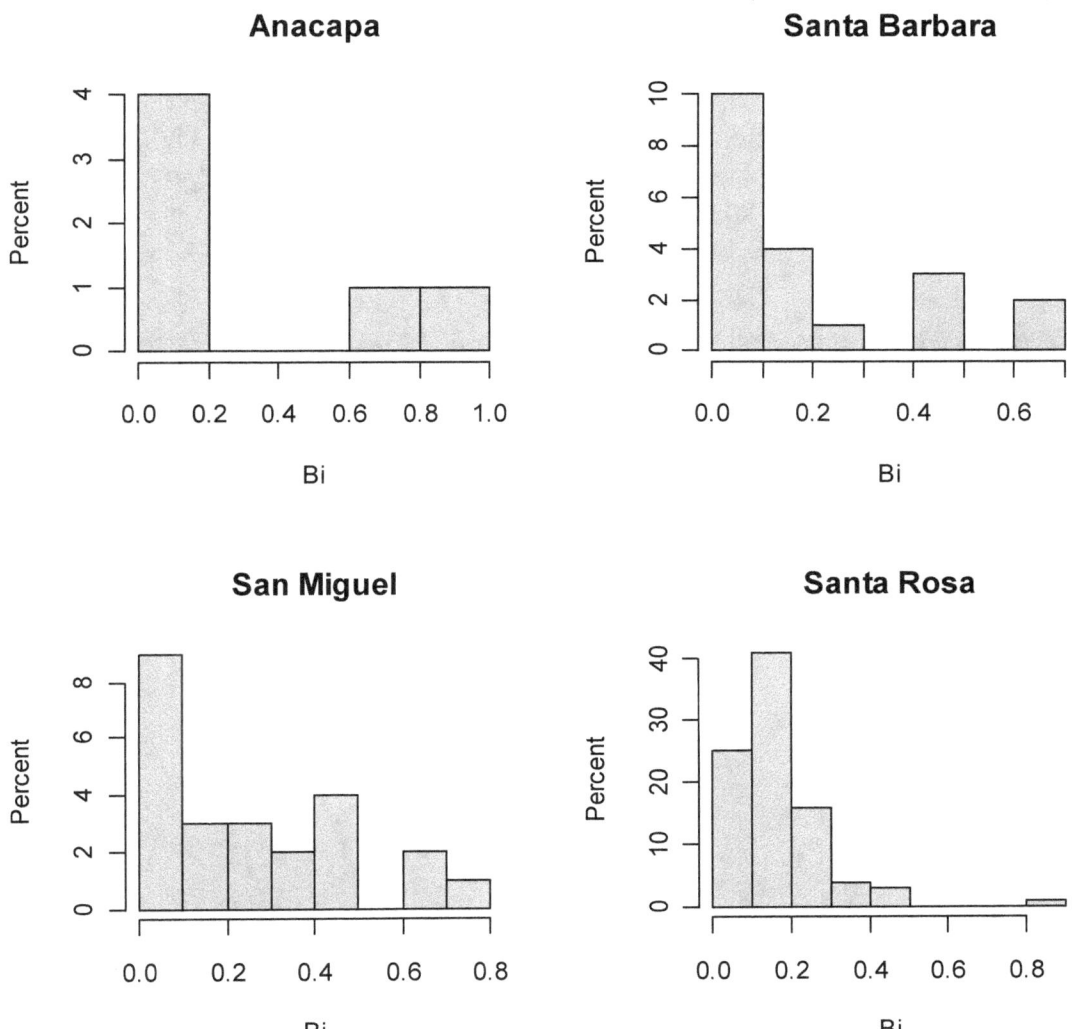

Figure 25. Distribution of standardized habitat selection ratios (Bi) for sixteen avian species on Anacapa, Santa Barbara, San Miguel, and Santa Rosa Islands, California from 1993 through 2008. The magnitude of the selection ratios tended to decrease on islands with greater number of habitats (e.g., most selection ratios on Santa Rosa were relatively low compared to those on other, smaller islands).

Trends for Species with Few Detections

Some information on trend, or at least presence/absence, is available for 5 species that had inadequate observations for density estimation (Table 10). Over the sampling period, European starlings all but disappeared from all four islands surveyed. Some starlings are observed annually in the Beecher's Bay ranch complex on Santa Rosa Island, though none have been observed during point count surveys. Observations of Hutton's vireos, mourning doves and northern mockingbirds on Santa Rosa, where they breed, were sporadic. All three were observed in highest numbers in 2006, the year in which the highest number of point count sites (199) were surveyed on that island.

Table 10. Number of individuals observed during landbird sampling for 6 species with inadequate number of detections to estimate density, 1993-2009.

Island	1993	1994	1995	1996	1997	1998	1999	2000	2001	2002	2003	2004	2005	2006	2007	2008	2009
Red-tailed hawk																	
AN		4		2	1	1											
SB			1														
SM	1	7	1	4	6	3		1	4	6	6	6	3	4	7	1	1
SR		2	1	5	3	2		10	5	6	6			21		9	7
Mourning dove																	
SR		12	2	4	6	4		1	1	1	1			18		2	8
Northern mockingbird																	
SR			1	1						2	1			22		11	10
Loggerhead shrike																	
SR		5		1		3		2		4				13		5	4
European starling																	
AN	48			25	1	1											
SB	5	18	26	1	4												
SM		91	2	12	1	19	6		8								
SR			9	36	3	3											
Hutton's vireo																	
SR				5		1				2				4			7

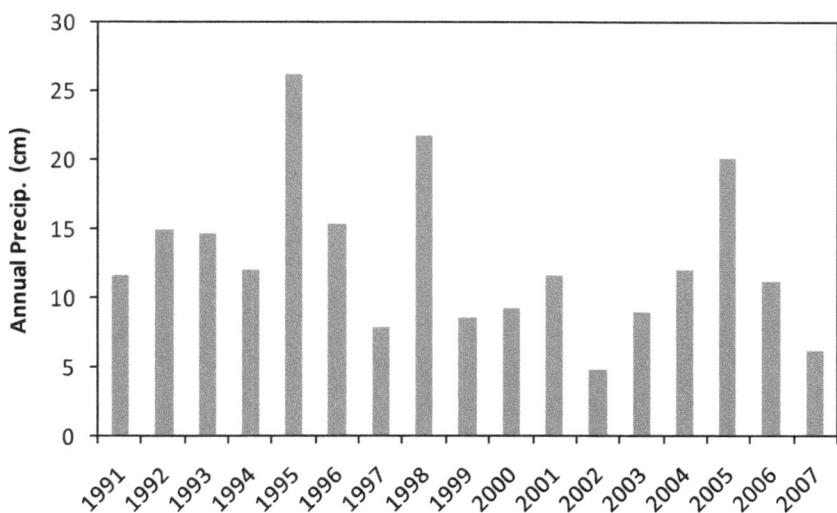

Figure 26. Annual precipitation (July-June) from the NPS remote area weather station (RAWS) on Black Mountain, Santa Rosa Island.

41

Discussion

Point count densities were generally higher than those from line transects, perhaps because of higher detectabilities (i.e., less pre-count flushing of birds) at distances close to the observer (Marsden 1999). Point counts had the additional advantage of being tied to vegetation (habitat) type, which enabled investigation of habitat utilization. Conversely, line transects crossed many vegetation types, and were not randomly located, which limits inferences about habitat use and selection from the results.

Landbird densities from both line transects and point counts were characterized by substantial interannual variability. Landbird populations, in general, exhibit high interannual variability (Taylor et al. 1994), due to the effects of annual differences in climatic variables such as precipitation and temperature on demographic variables such as individual survival and reproductive success. Although the Mediterranean climate of the Channel Islands is mild due to the periodic occurrence of the El Nino-Southern Oscillation, there is considerable annual variation in precipitation (Fig. 26). Such variation could drive population dynamics for some landbird species on the islands.

Inter-island climatic variability could also account for some differences in landbird densities between islands. For example, Santa Barbara Island, in the southeast portion of the archipelago, is warmer and drier than the islands in the northwest. The latter are more subject to the cool maritime fog layer driven onshore by prevailing northwest winds, and the fog layer is also a source of moisture in the form of fog drip, as captured by vegetation. Horned larks and western meadowlarks showed higher variability on Santa Barbara Island than on San Miguel, perhaps because of greater climatic variability on Santa Barbara. On the other hand, the presence of a predator, the island fox, may dampen landbird population cycles on San Miguel, though those two bird species did not increase on San Miguel after island foxes were removed from the wild for captive breeding (see below).

43

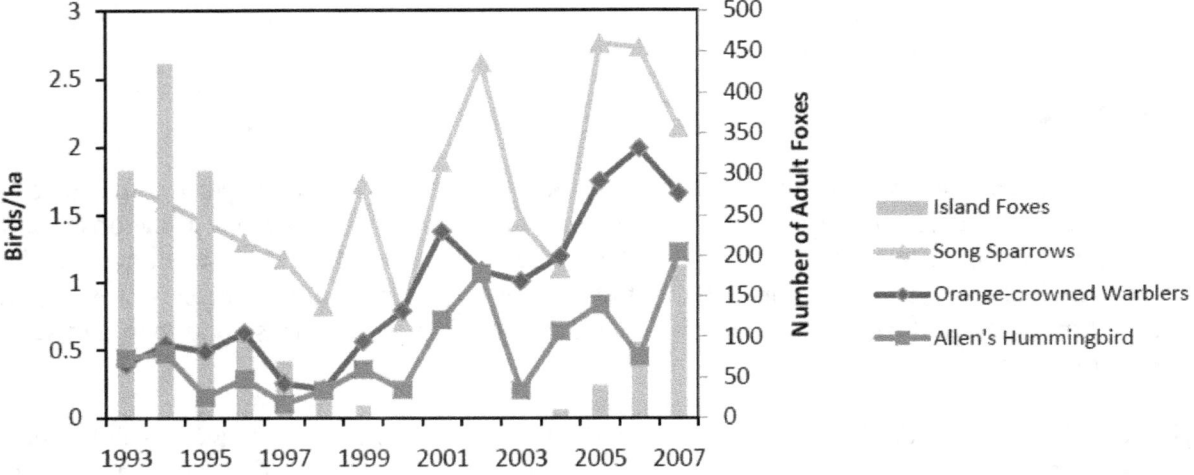

Figure 27. Changes in density on San Miguel of 3 bird species with estimated population size of island foxes, which were removed from the wild from 1999-2004 for captive breeding. Bird data are from line transects.

Density of Allen's hummingbirds, song sparrows and orange-crowned warblers on San Miguel Island seemed to be related to changes in density of island foxes, one of the few nest predators on the islands (Fig. 27). Island foxes existed at high population levels on San Miguel (>400) and Santa Rosa (>1000) in the early 1990s (Roemer et al. 1994). Golden eagle predation caused a rapid and deep decline in those populations, as well as for Santa Cruz Island foxes, in the mid-1990s, and the remaining foxes were captured and brought into captive breeding facilities in 1999-2000 (Coonan et al. 2005). Foxes were released back into the wild from 2003-2008 on Santa Rosa and 2004-2007 on San Miguel, and those wild populations subsequently increased (Fig. 27). Line transect landbird density data from San Miguel (1993-2007) bracket the period of fox decline, removal for captive breeding, and release back to the wild. Three landbird species that were stable or slightly declining prior to removal of foxes from the wild subsequently increased, with greater interannual variation, in a multi-year cycle (Fig. 27). There are no trees on San Miguel, and foxes are likely very effective nest predators. Collins and Laughrin (1979) found that birds occurred in 22% of San Miguel island fox fecal samples during spring, and comprised 13% of fox diet during that time period. Island fox predation can destroy up to ¼ of island song sparrow nestlings on San Miguel (Sogge and van Riper 1988), and consequently song sparrows on that island locate their nests deep within shrubs (Kern et al. 1993).

Removal of island foxes from the wild from 1999-2004 may have released these particular bird species from predation pressure. Their populations were no longer limited by predation, but may have fluctuated instead according to climatic and food variability. The effect of fox predation on birds may be more pronounced on San Miguel, where there are no other predators, such as spotted skunks or Santa Cruz Island jays, and where there is less shrub cover and no trees. In contrast, Santa Cruz Island has both island skunks (*Spilogale gracilis amphiala*) and jays, and greater tree and shrub cover than San Miguel. Occurrence of birds in island fox scat on that island was less (3-4%; Crooks and Van Vuren 1995) than on San Miguel.

That orange-crowned warblers on San Miguel experienced release from predation during fox removal is supported by recent work indicating that orange-crowned warblers on the Channel Islands adjust nest height according to perceived predation threat (Peluc et al 2008). During our

44

study, densities of orange-crowned warblers increased on San Miguel but also initially increased on Santa Barbara and Anacapa Islands (Fig. 16a), perhaps in response to climatic variability and food resources, although the increase was not sustained throughout the study period as it was on San Miguel. Orange-crowned warblers did not increase on Santa Rosa Island after removal of island foxes for captive breeding in 2000 (Fig. 16b). One reason that orange-crowned warblers did not increase on Santa Rosa may be because island spotted skunks, which do not occur on San Miguel, increased on Santa Rosa when foxes declined (NPS, unpubl. data). Spotted skunks are carnivorous (Crooks and Van Vuren 1995) and likely take bird eggs and nestlings.

On San Miguel, song sparrows and Allen's hummingbirds both showed much higher amplitude in interannual variation and a shift to multi-year cycles in the absence of foxes. Such shifts can occur when generalist predators, like the island fox, are removed from systems. Deer mice (*Peromyscus maniculatus*) on San Miguel showed a similar trend after foxes were brought into captivity (C. Drost, USGS Biological Resources Division, unpubl. data). Deer mice themselves can be effective predators of bird eggs on the Channel Islands. On Santa Barbara Island, deer mouse predation can account for up to 30% annual egg loss in a crevice-nesting alcid, the Xantus's murrelet (*Synthliboramthus hypoleucus*) (Schwemm and Martin 2005). Deer mouse numbers increased considerably on San Miguel following loss of foxes before falling to record lows (NPS, unpubl. data), and some of the fluctuation in bird numbers may have been due to egg predation by mice (Coonan et al. 2010).

As previously mentioned, two ground-nesting species, horned larks and western meadowlarks, did not increase after foxes were removed. The two species differ in their nesting requirements, with horned larks using relatively dry areas with sparse grass or forbs, and western meadowlarks nesting in thick grass (Shuford 1993). Because these two species did not increase following fox removal, predation may not have been a limiting factor for them.

Removal of foxes may have allowed one raptor species to begin breeding on the northern Channel Islands. During the period when island foxes were in captivity and absent from the wild, ground-nesting northern harriers began nesting on San Miguel and Santa Rosa Islands (C. Drost, USGS Biological Resources Division, unpubl. data); they had not been previously known to nest on the islands. Point count data suggests that northern harrier abundance declined on San Miguel after foxes were reintroduced to the wild in 2004 (Fig. 7b).

Expected Changes on Santa Rosa Island after Cattle Removal

Significant ecological changes occurred on Santa Rosa Island during the study period, and we expected landbird distribution and abundance to reflect some of those changes. Prior to the arrival of non-native ungulates in the 19th century, native shrub and tree cover on Santa Rosa was likely much greater than it is today. Due to over a century of uninterrupted grazing by feral pigs, cattle, horses, elk (*Cervus elaphus*) and deer (*Odooileus hemionus*), Santa Rosa's vegetation has been recently dominated by non-native annual grasslands, which covered approximately 80% of the island in 1990 (Clark et al. 1990). The island's streams and riparian areas were grazed intensively by cattle, and water quality was impacted to the point that the park was issued a cleanup or abatement order by the regional local water quality control board in 1995. The NPS removed feral pigs from Santa Rosa in 1992, and cattle were removed in 1998 as part of a court settlement. Deer and elk are now managed at lower numbers and will be removed from the island altogether by 2012, also as part of that court settlement. Removal or decrease in non-native ungulates has resulted in recovery of riparian areas (Wagner et al. 2004) and increased cover by native grasses and shrubs (D. Rodriguez, NPS, unpubl. data). Point count sampling in most habitats on Santa Rosa did not begin until 2001, but riparian areas have been well-sampled since 1994.

We expected to see increases in abundance of landbird species on Santa Rosa, particularly those which frequent riparian areas.However, there were surprisingly few increases in landbirds on Santa Rosa Island. Spotted towhees appeared to increase late in the study period (after 2000), while chipping sparrows increased early in the study period, after pigs were removed but before cattle were removed. Lesser goldfinches showed high variability but had their highest density values in 2006 and 2008. Western meadowlarks increased over the study period, perhaps reflecting an increase in productivity and diversity in grasslands, following cessation of cattle grazing and removal of pigs. Black phoebes actually declined islandwide and in riparian areas, for unknown reasons. Black phoebes are not in decline in California or elsewhere in the U.S., and have increased in California's central valley over the last few decades (Sauer et al. 2008).

Habitat Use

Although the line transect data could not be analyzed by habitat type, relative abundance from point count data revealed patterns of complex habitat utilization for some species. However, these results should be interpreted cautiously because the point count stations were not stratified proportional to habitat type. In addition, we are assuming that a bird recorded at a station was in the habitat associated with that station, which may not always be the case. It may be worthwhile to have observers record the habitat type in which they observe (or hear) a bird. Also the analysis with data pooled across islands may have overestimated selectivity because not all habitats were available to all species, and the results are likely being driven by patterns on Santa Rosa because that island had almost all of the species and the most point count stations.

For the 15 species evaluated for habitat use, landbird diversity generally increased with increasing structural complexity of the vegetation. Although landbird species richness was equivalent for all habitats but bare ground, iceplant and bluff habitat types (see Table 8 and Fig. 22), as Renyi's alpha increased (i.e. as the more abundant species had a greater influence on the measure of diversity, and rare species contributed less to diversity), woodland, riparian, pine and chaparral had higher bird diversity. The interpretation of this pattern is quite straightforward: woodland, riparian, pine and chaparral had the highest number of species and the distribution of abundance among them was relatively equitable, with few if any common species driving the diversity pattern. In contrast, grassland and scrub had similar numbers of species as woodland, riparian, pine and chaparral, but they were dominated by a few species; thus diversity in those habitats was not as equitable as in woodland, riparian, pine and chaparral.

Among the different island habitats, riparian areas and grasslands recorded, overall, the most observations and highest number of individual species (46 and 43 respectively; Fig. 28). The value of riparian areas to breeding birds is well-established, and bird diversity is generally higher in riparian areas (Stauffer and Best 1980, Knopf and Samson 1994) due to greater diversity in vegetation and structure. This is especially true in the arid southwestern United States, where riparian areas comprise a relatively small proportion of the landscape yet have disproportionately high bird diversity (Szaro 1980).

The high diversity in grasslands was more surprising. Grasslands, being structurally simple, generally have lower bird species diversity than other more complex habitats (MacArthur 1964). On the Channel Islands, however, areas identified as grassland habitat are not necessarily structurally simple. All the islands are gradually recovering from the effects of grazing, and some grasslands once dominated by alien annuals are being invaded by native bunchgrasses and shrubs.

The apparently high diversity in grasslands may be partially explained by the greater sampling effort in that habitat type. The 61 grassland point count sites are the most for any habitat type, and over all habitat types the number of species detected increased with the number of point count sites in a habitat type (Fig. 28). Given that, a relatively greater number of species were observed in riparian and coastal sage scrub communities. Moreover, as we mentioned above, diversity patterns in the grasslands were dominated by just a few species.

Among the 15 species for which we evaluated habitat use, few were habitat specialists. The average number of habitat types in which a species occurred was 6.4, and each species occurred in at least 5 habitat types. This is not unexpected, because compared to their mainland counterparts, island species occupy more habitat types (Blondel et al. 1988), due to fewer number of competing species, higher densities, and resultant niche expansion.

Almost all the species showed preferences for 3 or 4 habitat types. The two exceptions were black phoebes and horned larks, each of which showed strong preference for only one habitat type, riparian and grassland, respectively. Such species, which are apparently restricted to one habitat type, may be more vulnerable to effects of climate change, if their preferred habitats decline in area due to change in precipitation/temperature regimes. Black phoebes are widely distributed in coastal California, and south through Mexico, but horned larks on the islands are considered a separate subspecies, perhaps increasing their vulnerability.

Some species which occurred on multiple islands showed different habitat preferences on Santa Rosa Island than on smaller San Miguel and/or Santa Barbara. For example, orange-crowned warblers preferred scrub and grassland on all three islands, but on Santa Rosa also preferred chaparral and riparian habitat types. Western meadowlarks preferred grassland on all three islands but added coastal scrub on Santa Rosa. Other species, such as endemic horned larks and endemic song sparrows, had consistent habitat preferences across islands, even when more habitat types were available on the larger Santa Rosa.

For some species we noted specific differences between island and mainland habitat utilization. On Santa Rosa orange-crowned warblers preferred coastal sage scrub, grassland and chaparral and avoided closed-cone pine and oak woodland. Gilbert et al. (2010) report that orange-crowned warblers on the Channel Islands prefer humid and shaded sites on slopes, in canyons gullies and sea-cliffs in chaparral, Torrey pine, coastal bluff and coastal sage scrub vegetation types. Mainland orange-crowned warblers are ground-nesters, but island orange-crowned warblers nest on the ground as well as in shrubs and trees, with choice likely driven by perceived predation threat (Peluc et al. 2008). Grazing history on Santa Rosa Island may have left many otherwise dense habitat types in condition less desirable to species requiring concealment from predators.

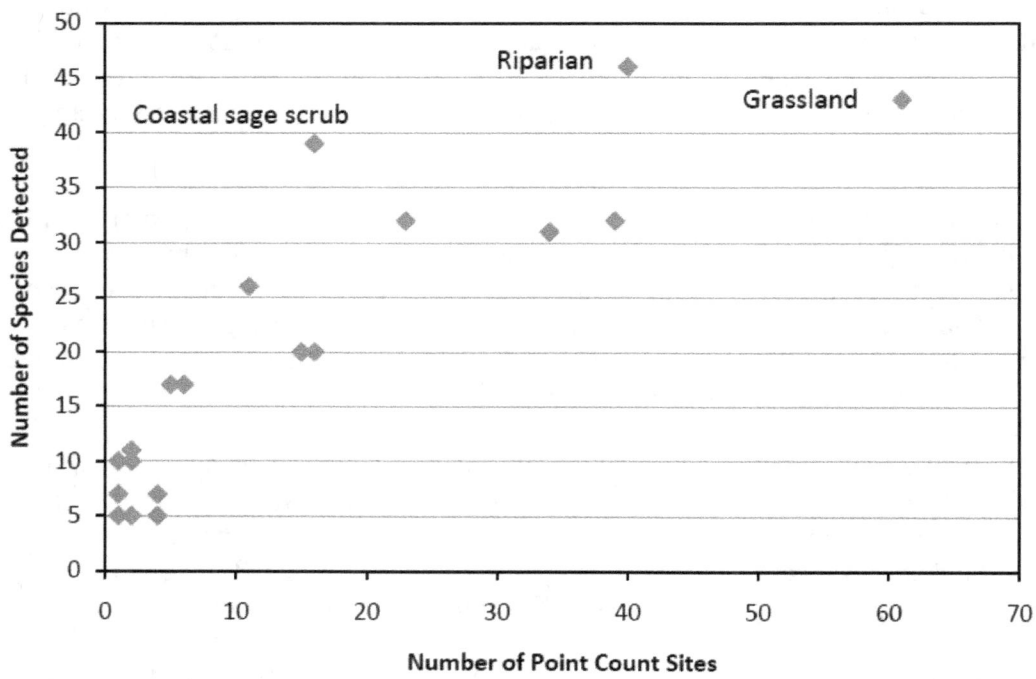

Figure 28. Relationship of number of species detected to number of point count sites in each habitat type., Channel Islands National Park, 1994-2009.

Song sparrows are distributed widely in North America and occur in many different habitat types, most often inhabiting shrubs on moist ground near freshwater, saltwater or coastline (Arcese et al. 2002). On San Miguel song sparrows have been found to be most abundant in areas with dense shrubs, and unlike on the mainland, were found in areas well-removed from water (Sogge and van Riper 1998), perhaps due to the availability of considerable fog-moisture on San Miguel. Song sparrow use of Santa Rosa habitats was also not tied to water availability. Song sparrow utilized riparian areas but did not prefer them. They strongly selected for coastal sage scrub and grassland, while avoiding chaparral, woodland and pine habitat types.

Western meadowlarks showed strong preference for grassland and coastal sage scrub. On the mainland meadowlarks inhabit grassland habitats, and avoid tall and dense vegetation (Davis and Lanyon 2008). It may be that coastal sage scrub on Santa Rosa Island retains considerable patches of both native and non-native grassland.

Other Trends

Some individual species showed trends which may have been related to other ecosystem-wide changes. American Kestrels declined, perhaps due to increases in island populations of peregrine falcons (*F. peregrinus*), which, as elsewhere in North America, had declined due to organochlorine pesticide contamination, but were successfully reintroduced to the Channel Islands in the 1980s and 1990s. American kestrels apparently disappeared from San Miguel and Santa Rosa Islands by 2008, and none were observed on those islands in 2009, though there were 2 observations on Santa Barbara Island (NPS, unpubl. data). Although peregrines have generally recovered on the islands (as elsewhere; they were removed from the federal list of endangered species in 1999), current numbers on the islands are unknown. Observations of peregrines from the landbird monitoring program are spotty and variable, and do not suggest an increase during the period of kestrel decline on Santa Rosa and San Miguel.

The increase in common ravens on San Miguel and Santa Rosa Islands, although concurrent with the removal of island foxes from the wild, may instead be related to changes in carrion availability, perhaps due to changes in ungulate management on Santa Rosa Island or in changes in island pinniped populations. Ravens began increasing on San Miguel in 2001, with a spike in 2007. The increase on Santa Rosa was of lower magnitude, more gradual, and appeared to exhibit fluctuation. The populations of mule deer and elk on Santa Rosa Island have been managed more rigorously since 1999, and possibly greater availability of carrion from the annual trophy hunt and cull has supported an increased raven population. It is more likely, though, that increased raven populations are tied to raven exploitation of pinniped carcasses on San Miguel. Robert Delong of the National Marine Fisheries Service reports that ravens arrived on San Miguel in the 1980s and began scavenging on pinnipeds in the 1990s, when mortality caused by hookworm (*Uncinaria* spp.) substantially increased the number of carcasses of California sea lion (*Zalophus californianus*) pups, and ravens learned to open carcasses (R. Delong, NMFS-Alaska Science Center, unpubl. data). Ravens may also take advantage of even larger carrion. Several hundred ravens were observed in the immediate area of a blue whale (*Balaenoptera musculus*) carcass on San Miguel Island (D. Richards, NPS, pers. comm.).

Apparent trends for some other species are not readily explained. European starlings, an alien species, were regularly observed on all four islands during the 1990s, but had practically disappeared from all four by 2001. Rock wrens all but disappeared from San Miguel Island, for unknown reasons. House finches, which had been observed primarily on the Nidever Canyon transect on San Miguel Island, declined to very low numbers on that island for 5-6 years, but by 2008-2009 had begun to recover (total observed annually for 2006-2009 was, 5, 7, 12 and 32, respectively). Point count data indicated that western meadowlarks declined on Santa Barbara and San Miguel Islands from 2001-2008, though line transect data do not indicate such a decline.

Some species which breed on Santa Rosa (Hutton's vireo, mourning dove, and northern mockingbird) were observed so rarely that the number of records was insufficient to construct detectability curves and estimate density. Over time, however, the cumulative number of records will increase to the point where density estimation is possible. Because the sampling effort on Santa Rosa has increased with the shift to point-count sampling, sustained sampling on that island will likely return adequate trend data for these species within several years.

Two species recently observed on Santa Rosa may eventually be found to breed on that island. Bushtits and acorn woodpeckers are common residents on Santa Cruz Island, but the former is not known from Santa Rosa and the latter is known only as a rare winter visitor to the island (Jones et al. 1985). Low numbers of each species have been recorded on Santa Rosa point counts since 2008, in riparian or woodland habitats. Post-grazing recovery of those habitat types may support breeding by those species.

In the future it may be interesting to look at specific trends in the few habitat types that have sufficient point count sites ($\geq$ 10) to do so (grassland on Santa Barbara, San Miguel and Santa Rosa; coastal sage scrub, chaparral, mixed woodland, riparian and Torrey pine on Santa Rosa). Complete or nearly-complete sampling was only conducted in those habitat types for 4 of the 15 years included in this study (2003, 2004, 2006, 2008).

Conclusion

The park's landbird monitoring program, one of the longest-running landbird population monitoring programs in the U.S., provided trend data for half of the park's 44 known breeding landbird species. Density estimates from distance sampling could be constructed for 18 species, and presence/absence data was available for an additional 5 species. The methods were incapable of detecting trends for rare species such as the island loggerhead shrike, for owls, and some large raptors such as bald and golden eagles and peregrine falcons. The park's monitoring program was established prior to NPS partial ownership of Santa Cruz Island, and so does not provide information on landbird species such as the endemic island scrub-jay which, at least in the park, breed only on that island. Distance sampling methods allow estimation of density and are robust to observer variability, due to incorporation of covariates in the model; problems with confidence intervals and annual variability are lessened over time, as the number of detections for each species accrues. However, transect or point-count based methods provide little information on trends for rare species, which require more intensive localized monitoring, such as area searches. The shift to point counts after a 2001 program review allowed evaluation of landbird use of habitat, though line transect monitoring on the three smaller islands, which have less topographical and vegetation diversity, returned interesting trends related to ecological changes on those islands, with acceptably low coefficients of variation in probability density function.

Literature Cited

Arcese, P., M.K. Sogge, A.B. Marr and M.A. Patten. 2002. Song Sparrow (*Melospiza melodia*), The Birds of North America Online (A. Poole, Ed.). Ithaca: Cornell Lab of Ornithology; Retrieved from the Birds of North America Online: http://bna.birds.cornell.edu/bna/species/704

Beason, R.C. 1995. Horned Lark (*Eremophila alpestris*), The Birds of North America Online (A. Poole, Ed.). Ithaca: Cornell Lab of Ornithology; Retrieved from the Birds of North America Online: http://bna.birds.cornell.edu/bna/species/195

Blondel, J., D. Chessel and B. Frochot. 1988. Bird species impoverishment, niche expansion, and density inflation in Mediterranean island habitats. Ecology 69(6):1899-1917.

Buckland, S.T., D.R. Anderson, K.P. Burnham, J.L. Laake, D.L. Borchers, and L. Thomas. 2001. Introduction to distance sampling: estimating abundance of biological populations. Oxford University Press, Oxford, UK.

Clark, R.A., W.L. Halvorson, A.A. Sawdo and K.C. Danielsen. 1990. Plant communities of Santa Rosa Island, Channel Islands National Park. Cooperative Park Studies Unit, University of California, Davis. Technical Report 42. 93 pages.

Collins, P.W. 1999. Rufous-crowned Sparrow (*Aimophila ruficeps*), The Birds of North America Online (A. Poole, Ed.). Ithaca: Cornell Lab of Ornithology; Retrieved from the Birds of North America Online: http://bna.birds.cornell.edu/bna/species/472

Collins, P.W. and B.C. Latta. 2006. Nesting season diet of golden eagles on Santa Cruz and Santa Rosa Islands, Santa Barbara County, California. Santa Barbara Museum of Natural History Technical Reports – No. 3.

Collins, P.W., and L.L. Laughrin. 1979. Vertebrate zoology: the island fox on San Miguel Island. Pages 12.1-12.52 *in* Power, D.M., ed., Natural Resources Study of the Channel Islands National Monument, California. Prepared for the National Park Service, Denver Service Center by the Santa Barbara Museum of Natural History, Santa Barbara, California.

Coonan, T.J., K.A. Rutz, D.K. Garcelon, B.C. Latta, M.M. Gray, and E.T. Aschehoug. 2005. Progress in island fox recovery efforts on the northern Channel Islands. Pages 263-273 *in* Garcelon, D.K. and C.A. Schwemm, (eds.), Proceedings of the Sixth California Islands Symposium. National Park Service Technical Publication CHIS-05-01, Institute for Wildlife Studies, Arcata, CA.

Coonan, T.J., C.A. Schwemm and D.K. Garcelon. 2010. Decline and recovery of the island fox: a case study for population recovery. Cambridge University Press, Cambridge, UK.

Crooks, K.R. and D. Van Vuren. 1995. Resource utilization by two insular endemic mammalian carnivores, the island fox and island spotted skunk. Oecologia 104(3):301-307.

Davis, G.E., K.R. Faulkner and W.L. Halvorson. 1994. Ecological monitoring in Channel Islands National Park. Pages 465-484 *in* Halvorson, W.L. and G.J. Maender, eds., The Forth California Islands Symposium: Update on the Status of Resources. Santa Barbara Museum of Natural History, Santa Barbara, California.

Davis, Stephen K. and Wesley E. Lanyon. 2008. Western Meadowlark (*Sturnella neglecta*), The Birds of North America Online (A. Poole, Ed.). Ithaca: Cornell Lab of Ornithology; Retrieved from the Birds of North America Online: http://bna.birds.cornell.edu/bna/species/104

Delaney, K.S. and R.K. Wayne. 2005. Adaptive units for conservation: population distinction and historic extinctions in the island jay. Biological Conservation 19(2): 523-533.

Diamond, J.M. 1969. Avifaunal equilibria and species turnover rates on the Channel Islands of California. Proceedings of the National Academy of Sciences 64:57-63.

Eggert, L.S., N.I. Mundy and D.S. Woodruff. 2004. Population structure of loggerhead shrikes in the California Channel Islands. Molecular Ecology 13:2121-2133.

Gilbert, W. M., M. K. Sogge and C. Van Riper III. 2010. Orange-crowned Warbler (*Oreothlypis celata*), The Birds of North America Online (A. Poole, Ed.). Ithaca: Cornell Lab of Ornithology; Retrieved from the Birds of North America Online: http://bna.birds.cornell.edu/bna/species/101

Greenlaw, J.S. 1996. Spotted Towhee (*Pipilo maculatus*), The Birds of North America Online (A. Poole, Ed.). Ithaca: Cornell Lab of Ornithology; Retrieved from the Birds of North America Online: http://bna.birds.cornell.edu/bna/species/263

Hill, G.E. 1993. House Finch (*Carpodacus mexicanus*), The Birds of North America Online (A. Poole, Ed.). Ithaca: Cornell Lab of Ornithology; Retrieved from the Birds of North America Online: http://bna.birds.cornell.edu/bna/species/046

Hill, M.O. 1973. Diversity and evenness: a unifying notation and its consequences. Ecology 54 (2): 427-432.

Johnson, N.K. 1972. Origin and differentiation of the avifauna of the Channel Islands, California. Condor 74:295-315.

Jones, L., P. Collins and R. Stefani. 1999. A checklist of the birds of Channel Islands National Park. 2nd edition. Southwest Parks and Monuments Association, Tucson, Arizona.

Kennedy, E.D. and D.W. White. 1997. Bewick's Wren (*Thryomanes bewickii*), The Birds of North America Online (A. Poole, Ed.). Ithaca: Cornell Lab of Ornithology; Retrieved from the Birds of North America Online: http://bna.birds.cornell.edu/bna/species/315

Kern, M.D., M.K. Sogge, R.B. Kern and C. van riper III. 1993. Nests and nest sites of the San Miguel Island song sparrow. Journal of Field Ornithology 64:367-381.

Knopf, F.L. and F.B. Samson. 1994. Scale perspectives on avian diversity in western riparian ecosystems. Conservation Biology 8(3): 669-676.

Latta, B. C., D. E. Driscoll, J. L. Linthicum, R. E. Jackman and G. Doney. 2005. Capture and translocation of golden eagles from the California Channel Islands to mitigate depredation of endemic island foxes. Pages 341-350 *in* Garcelon, D. K., and C. A. Schwemm, eds., Proceedings of the Sixth California Islands Symposium. National Park Service Technical Publication CHIS-05-01, Institute for Wildlife Studies, Arcata, California.

Lynch, J.F. and N.K. Johnson. 1974. Turnover and equilibria in insular avifaunas, with special reference to the California Channel Islands. Condor 76:370-384.

Lowther, P.E. 2000. Pacific-slope Flycatcher (*Empidonax difficilis*), The Birds of North America Online (A. Poole, Ed.). Ithaca: Cornell Lab of Ornithology; Retrieved from the Birds of North America Online: http://bna.birds.cornell.edu/bna/species/556a

MacArthur, R.H. 1964. Environmental factors affecting bird species diversity. American Naturalist 98:387-397.

Manly, B.F., L. McDonald, D.L. Thomas, and T.L. McDonald and W.P. Erickson. 2002 Resource selection by animals: statistical design and analysis for field studies. Kluwer Academic Publishers, Dordrecht, The Netherlands.

Marsden, S.J. 1999. Estimation of parrot and hornbill densities using a point count distance sampling method. Ibis 141(3):327-390.

McKeachern, K. 2000. Channel Islands National Park landbird monitoring program review, April 18-19, 2000. U.S. Geological Survey, Biological Resources Division, Western Ecological Research Station. Unpublished report on file at headquarters, Channel Islands National Park, Ventura, California.

Middleton, A.L. 1998. Chipping Sparrow (*Spizella passerina*), The Birds of North America Online (A. Poole, Ed.). Ithaca: Cornell Lab of Ornithology; Retrieved from the Birds of North America Online: http://bna.birds.cornell.edu/bna/species/334

Mitchell, D.E. 2000. Allen's Hummingbird (*Selasphorus sasin*), The Birds of North America Online (A. Poole, Ed.). Ithaca: Cornell Lab of Ornithology; Retrieved from the Birds of North America Online: http://bna.birds.cornell.edu/bna/species/501

Peluc, S.I., T.S. Sillett, J.T. Rotenberry and C.K. Gahalambor. 2008. Adaptive phenotypic plasticity in an island songbird exposed to a novel predation risk. Behavioral Ecology 19:830-835.

Renyi, A.1961. On measures of entropy and information. P. 547-561 in J. Neyman, ed., 4th Berkeley symposium on mathematical statistics and probability. Volume I. University of California Press, Berkeley.

Sauer, J. R., J. E. Hines, and J. Fallon. 2008. The North American Breeding Bird Survey, Results and Analysis 1966 - 2007. Version 5.15.2008. USGS Patuxent Wildlife Research Center, Laurel, Maryland.

Schwemm, C.A. and P.L Martin. 2005. Response of nest success of Xantus' murrelet (*Synthliboranthus hypoleucus*) to native predator abundance, Santa Barbara Island, California. Pgs. 373-384 *in* Garcelon, D. K., and C. A. Schwemm, eds., Proceedings of the Sixth California Islands Symposium. National Park Service Technical Publication CHIS-05-01, Institute for Wildlife Studies, Arcata, California.

Shuford, W. D. 1993. The Marin County breeding bird atlas: a distributional and natural history of coastal California Birds. BushTit Books, Bolinas, California.

Sogge, M.K. and C. van Riper III. 1988. Breeding biology and population dynamics of the San Miguel Island song sparrow (*Melospiza melodia micronyx*). Technical Report Number 26, Cooperative National Park Resources Studies Unit, University of California, Davis.

Stanbury, A. and R. Gregory. 2009. Exploring the effects of truncated, pooled and sexed data in distance sampling estimation of breeding bird abundance. Bird Study 56(3):298–309.

Stauffer , F. and L.B. Best. 1980. Habitat selection by birds of riparian communities: evaluating effects of habitat alterations. Journal of Wildlife Management 44(1):, No. 1:1-15.

Super, P. E., C. van Riper III, and M. K. Sogge. 1991. Santa Rosa Island land bird monitoring handbook. Unpublished report on file at headquarters, Channel Islands National Park, Ventura, California.

Szaro, R.C. 1980. Factors influencing bird populations in Southwestern riparian forests [USA] . Pages 403-418 in R.M. DeGraff, tech. coord., Workshop on the Management of Western Forests and Grasslands for Nongame Birds, Salt Lake City (USA), 1980. USDA Forest Service general technical report INT-86, Ogden, Utah.

Taylor, D.M., D.F. DeSante, G.R. Geupel and K. Houghton. 1994. Autumn populations of landbirds along central coastal California 1976-1986. Journal of Field Ornithology 65(2):169-185.

Thomas, L., J.L. Laake, S. Strindberg, F.F.C. Marques, S.T. Buckland, D.L. Borchers, D.R. Anderson, K.P. Burnham, S.L. Hedley, J.H. Pollard and J.R.B. Bishop. 2003. Distance 4.1. Release 2. Research Unit for Wildlife Population Assessment, University of St. Andrews, UK, http://www.ruwpa.stand.ac.uk/distance/

Tothmeresz, B.1995. Comparison of different methods for diversity ordering. Journal of Vegetation Science 6(2): .83–290

van Riper, C., III, M. K. Sogge, and C. Drost. 1988. Land bird monitoring handbook, Channel Islands National Park, California. National Park Service, Ventura, California.

Wagner, J., M. Martin, K.r. Faulkner, S. Chaney, K. Noon, M. Denn and J. Reiner. 2004. Riparian system recovery after removal of livestock from Santa Rosa Island, Channel Islands National Park, California. Technical Report NPS/NRWRD/NRTR-2004/324. National Park Service Water Resources Division, Fort Collins, Colorado.

Appendix A   Detection Probability Plots

The following detection probability plots depict the attenuation of detectability as distance increases from the observer, for each species. Data are derived from the model selected in program Distance for either line transect or point count analyses (see Table 6). For line transects the x-axis represents perpendicular distance from transect midline, and the y-axis is detection probability. For point counts, x-axis represents distance from center of plot.

Line Transects

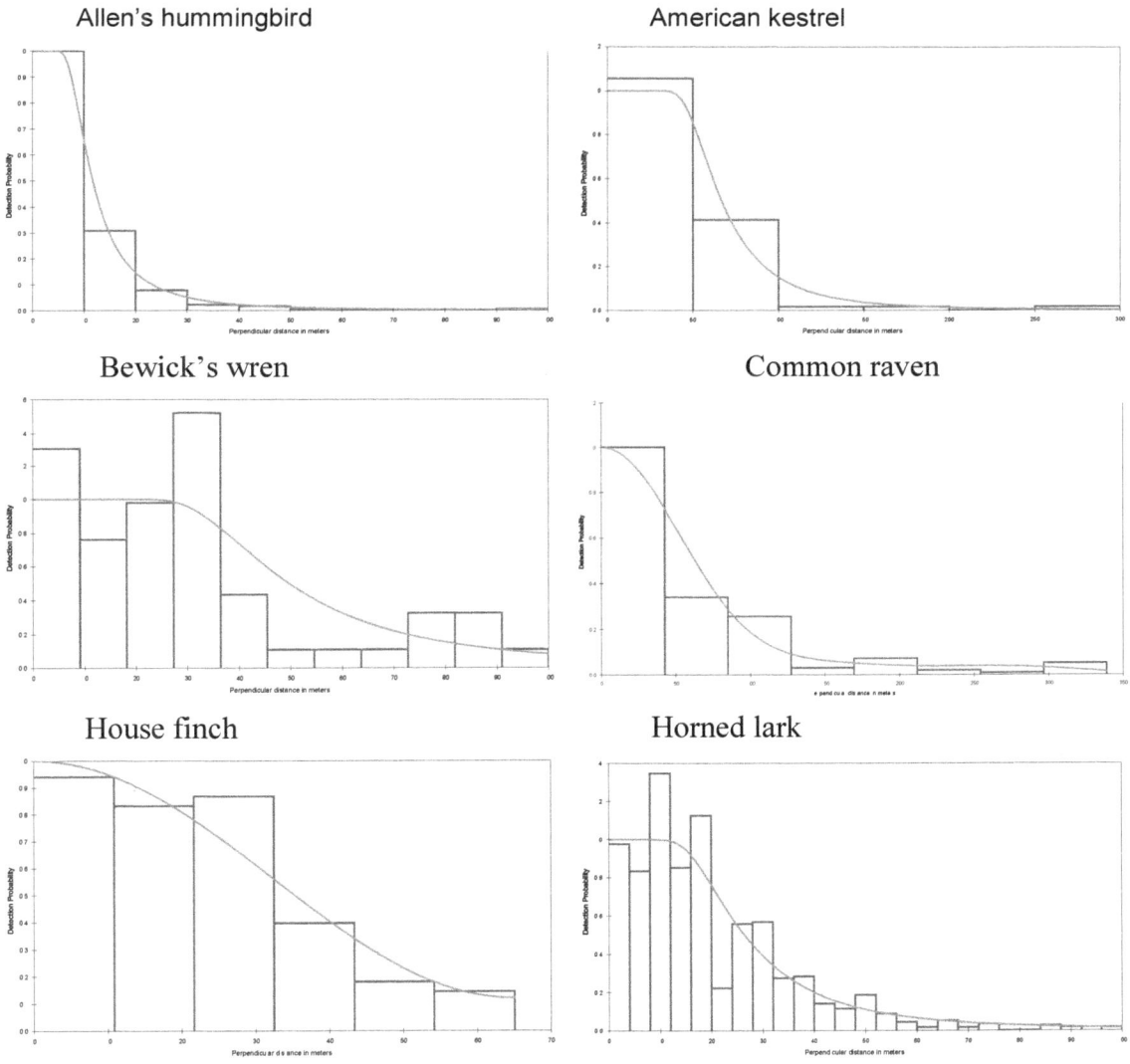

Song sparrow

Western meadowlark

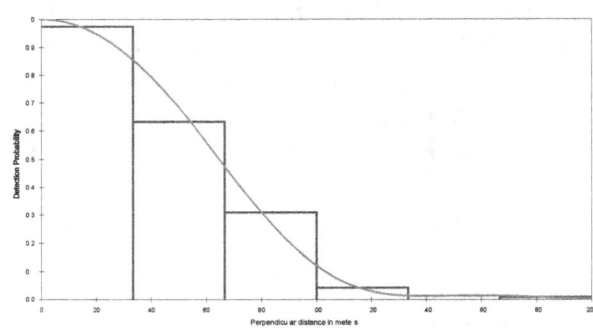

Rock Wren/Bewick's wren

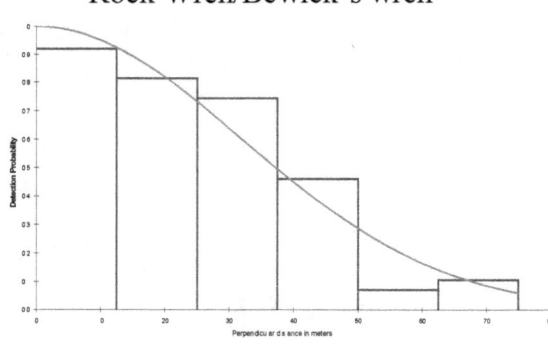

Northern harrier

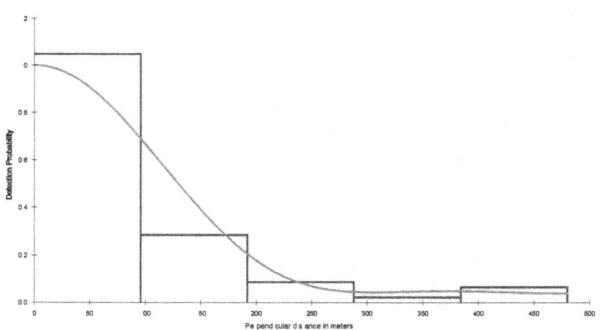

Orange-crowned warbler

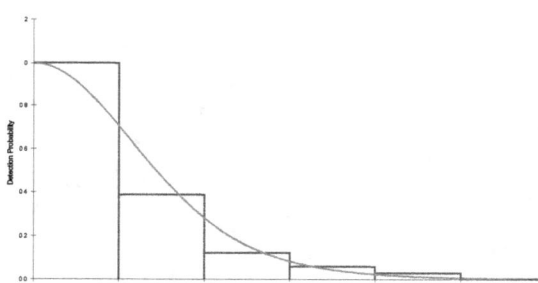

Point Counts

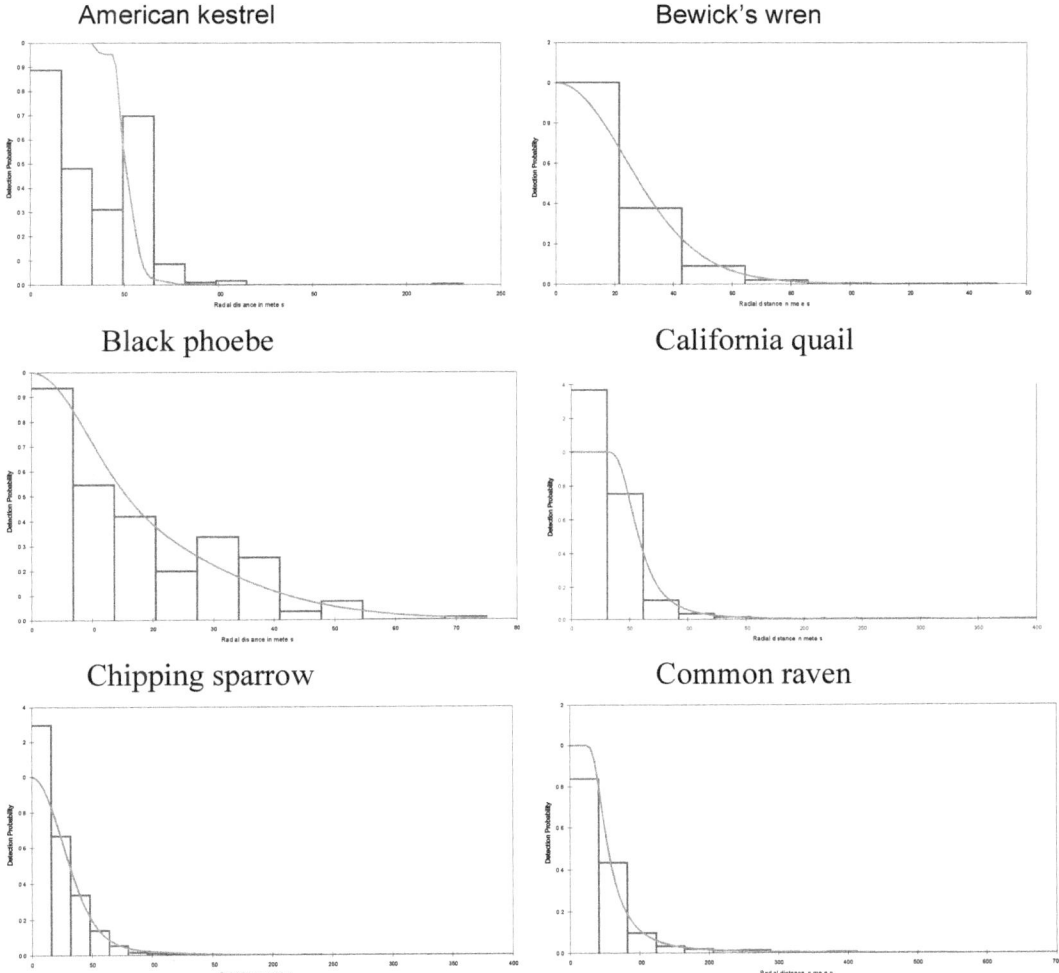

Lesser goldfinch

Orange-crowned warbler

Pacific-slope flycatcher

Rock wren

Song sparrow

Spotted towhee

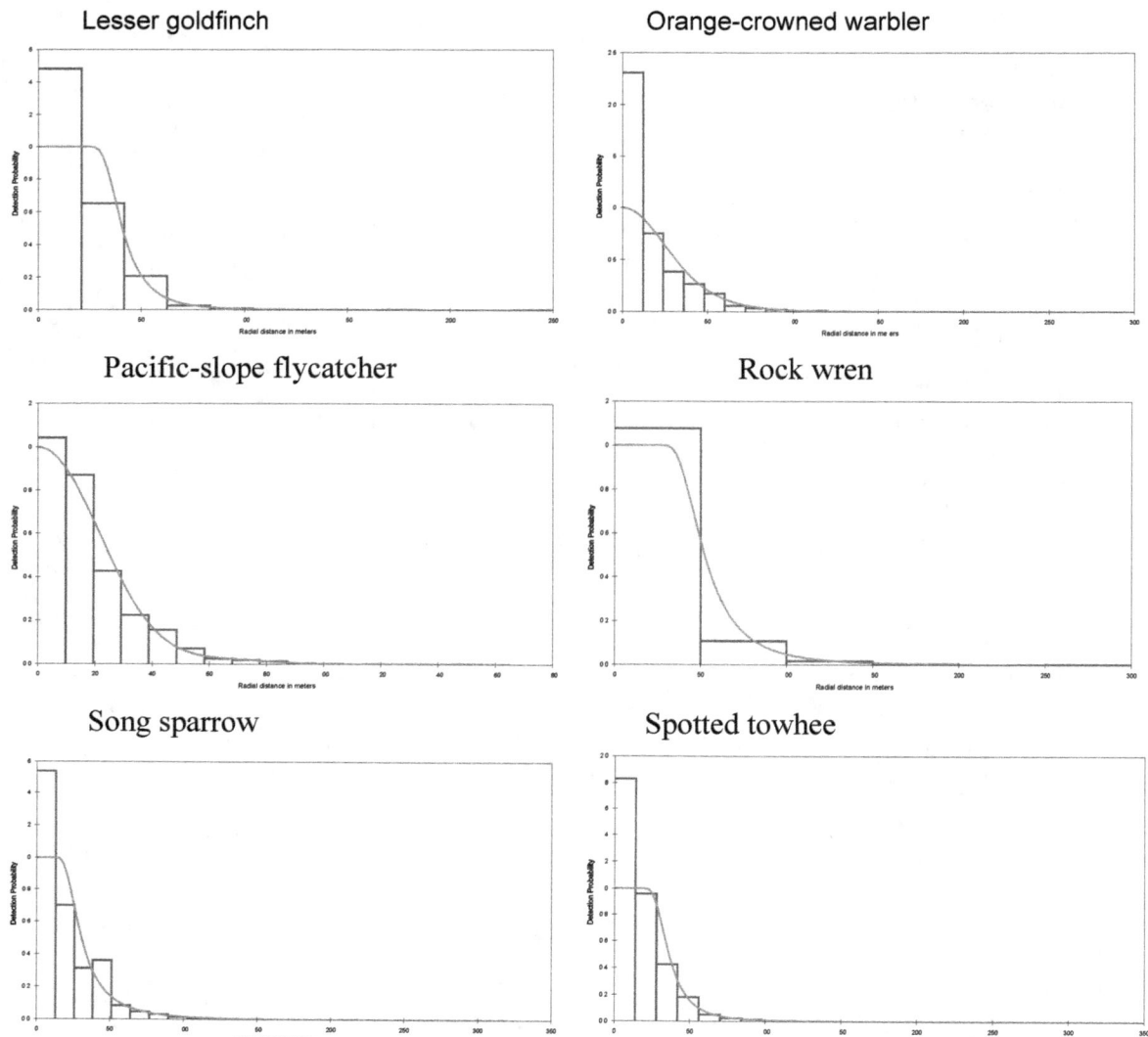

60

Anna's hummingbird

Northern harrier

Barn swallow

House finch

Horned lark

Western meadowlark

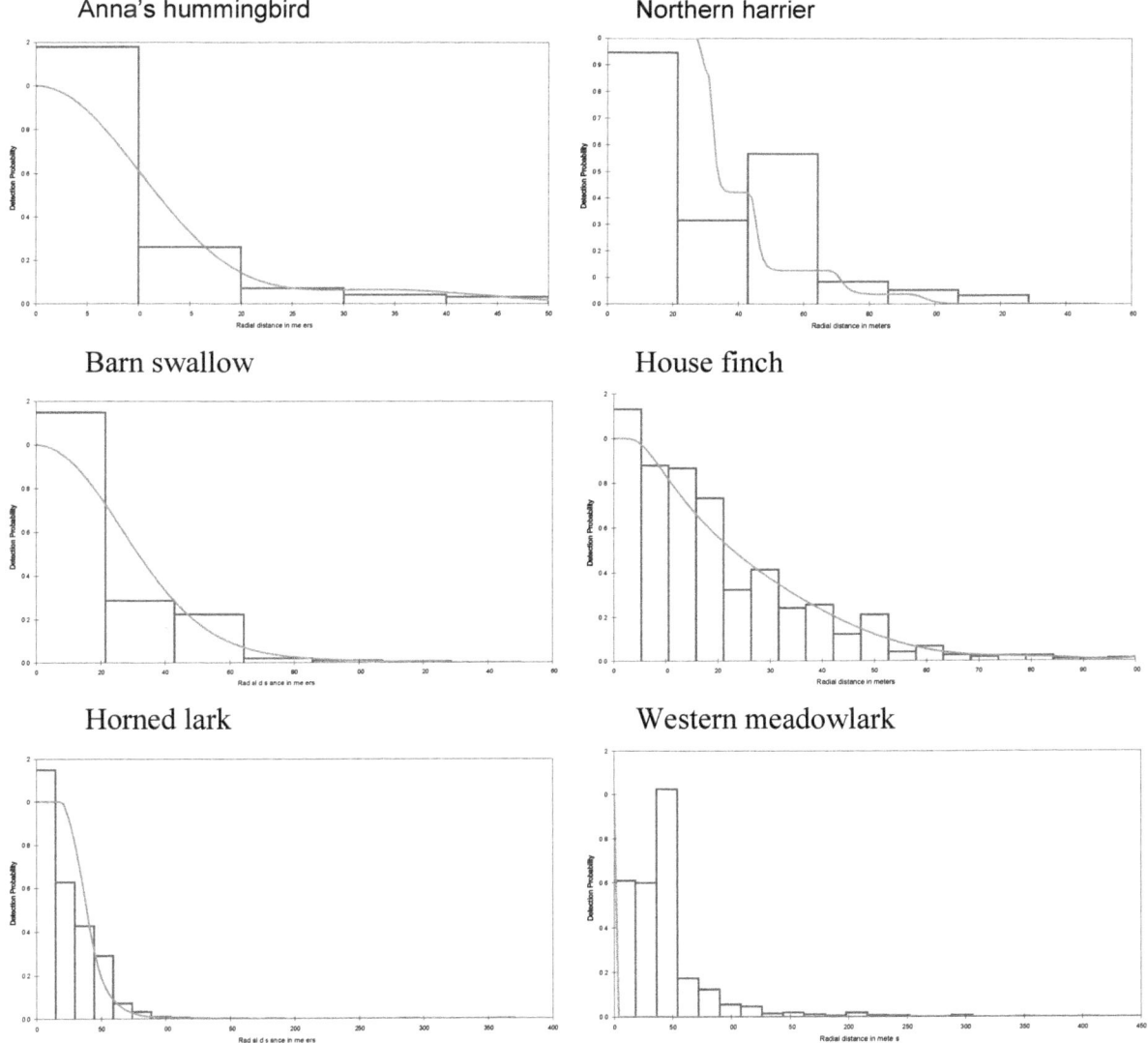

61

Allen's hummingbird

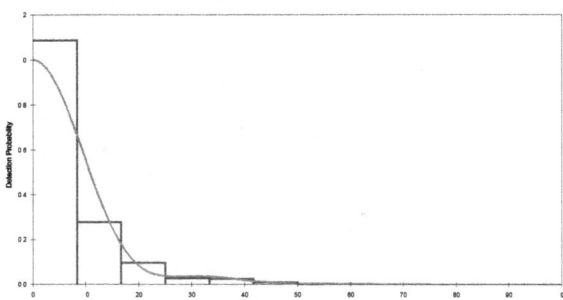

Appendix B   Comparison of Line Transect and Point Count Densities

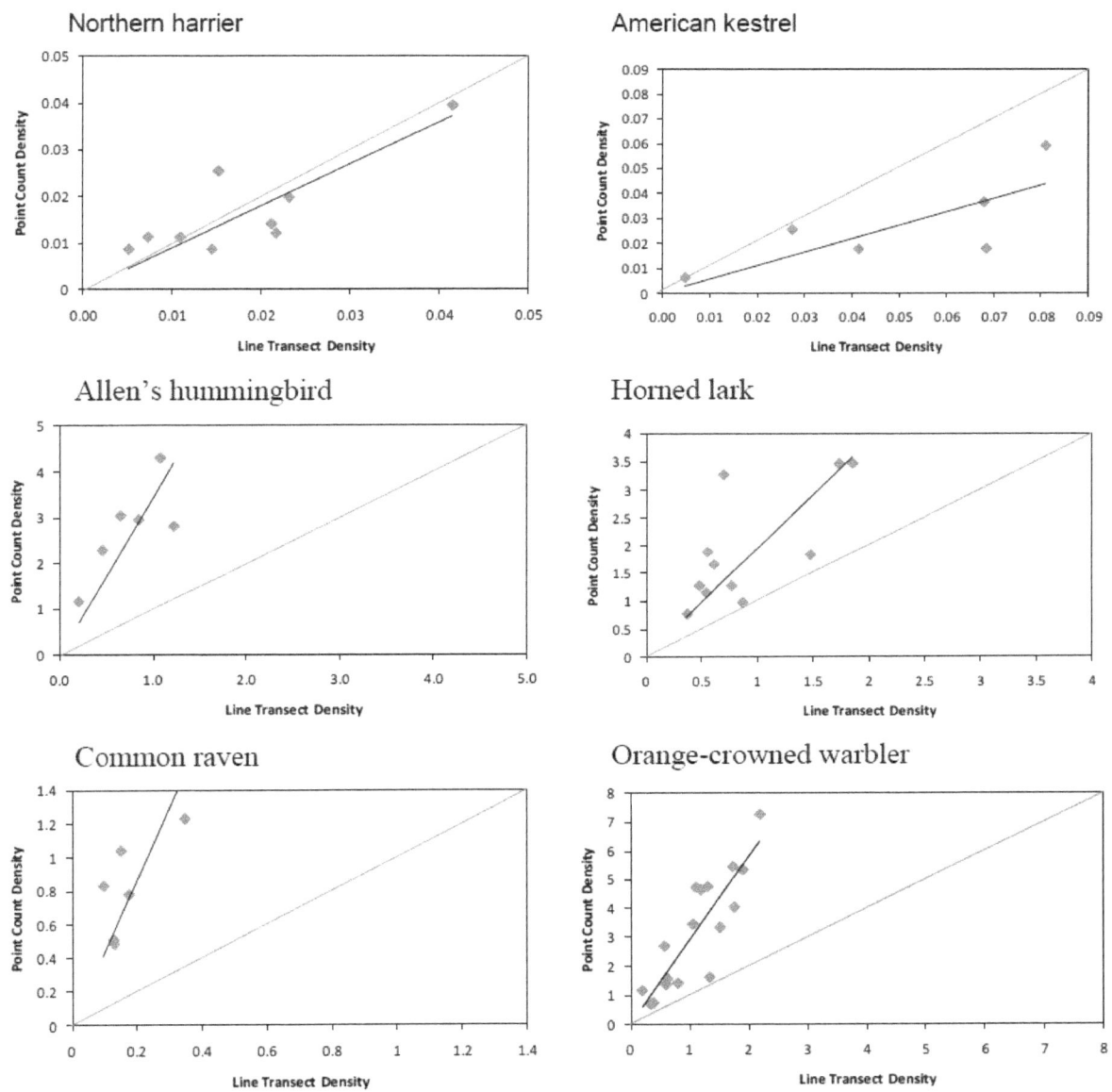

Song sparrow

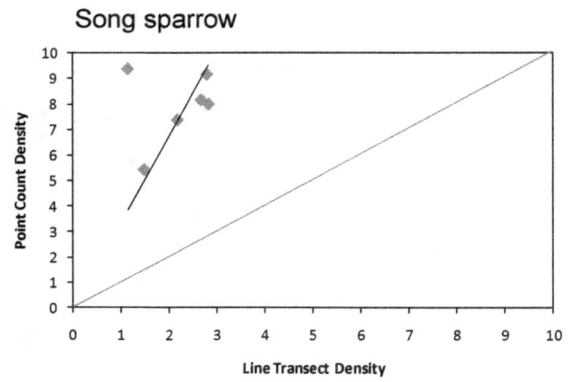

Western meadowlark

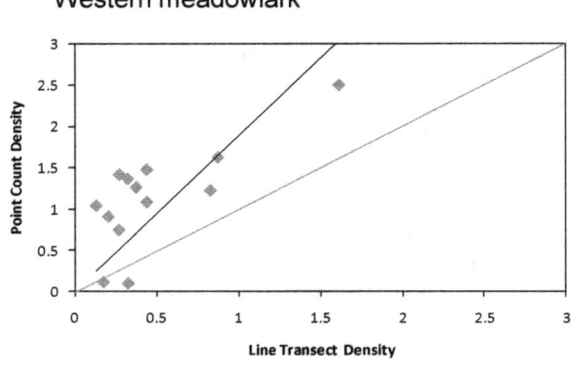

House finch

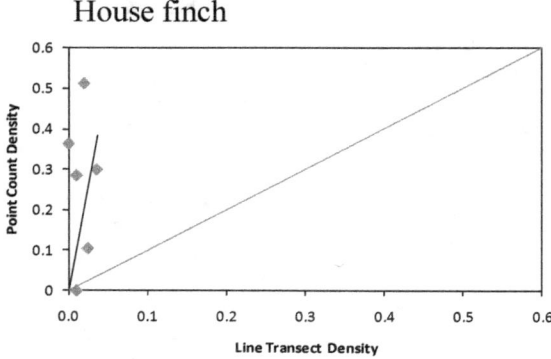

Appendix C   Standardized Habitat Selection Ratios for 15 Species

Standardized selection ratio, or B_i, is the proportional occurrence of a species in a habitat type, relative to the availability of that habitat type, and standardized to allow comparisons among habitat types. For example, California quail used chaparral fives times more than they use grassland (0.352 vs 0.071, below).

Habitat	*Bi*	*P*	Habitat	*Bi*	*P**
Allen's hummingbird			*California quail*		
Bare	0.000	0.0000	Bare	0.000	0.0000
Bluff	0.000	0.0000	Bluff	0.000	0.0000
Chaparral	0.191	0.0034	Chaparral	0.352	0.0014
Grassland	0.045	0.0000	Grassland	0.071	0.6484
Iceplant	0.000	0.0000	Iceplant	0.000	0.0000
Pine	0.275	0.0000	Pine	0.226	0.0401
Riparian	0.202	0.0000	Riparian	0.155	0.0073
Scrub	0.023	0.0000	Scrub	0.020	0.0000
Woodland	0.264	0.0000	Woodland	0.176	0.0412
Anna's hummingbird			*Chipping sparrow*		
Bare	0.000	0.0000	Bare	0.000	0.0000
Bluff	0.000	0.0000	Bluff	0.000	0.0000
Chaparral	0.235	0.0233	Chaparral	0.243	0.0000
Grassland	0.025	0.0001	Grassland	0.124	0.0001
Iceplant	0.000	0.0000	Iceplant	0.000	0.0000
Pine	0.328	0.0015	Pine	0.336	0.0000
Riparian	0.092	0.5215	Riparian	0.085	0.9760
Scrub	0.032	0.0000	Scrub	0.039	0.0000
Woodland	0.288	0.0001	Woodland	0.173	0.0000
Bewick's wren			*House finch*		
Bare	0.000	0.0000	Bare	0.000	0.0000
Bluff	0.000	0.0000	Bluff	0.000	0.0000
Chaparral	0.291	0.0000	Chaparral	0.244	0.0000
Grassland	0.046	0.0000	Grassland	0.058	0.0010
Iceplant	0.006	0.0000	Iceplant	0.000	0.0000
Pine	0.201	0.0000	Pine	0.325	0.0000
Riparian	0.185	0.0000	Riparian	0.133	0.0000
Scrub	0.018	0.0000	Scrub	0.026	0.0000
Woodland	0.252	0.0000	Woodland	0.215	0.0000

*compared to critical Bonferroni-adjusted level of 0.0056

Habitat	Bi	P	Habitat	Bi	P
Black phoebe			*Horned lark*		
Bare	0.000	0.0000	Bare	0.045	0.0000
Bluff	0.000	0.0000	Bluff	0.052	0.0000
Chaparral	0.056	0.1251	Chaparral	0.015	0.0000
Grassland	0.118	0.6138	Grassland	0.491	0.0000
Iceplant	0.000	0.0000	Iceplant	0.141	0.6935
Pine	0.056	0.1251	Pine	0.097	0.2223
Riparian	0.646	0.0000	Riparian	0.017	0.0000
Scrub	0.025	0.0000	Scrub	0.112	0.0334
Woodland	0.098	0.4362	Woodland	0.030	0.0000
Lesser goldfinch			*Song sparrow*		
Bare	0.000	0.0000	Bare	0.000	0.0000
Bluff	0.000	0.0000	Bluff	0.052	0.0000
Chaparral	0.329	0.0000	Chaparral	0.184	0.3352
Grassland	0.058	0.0739	Grassland	0.213	0.0001
Iceplant	0.000	0.0000	Iceplant	0.000	0.0000
Pine	0.257	0.0000	Pine	0.045	0.0000
Riparian	0.084	0.3847	Riparian	0.171	0.4704
Scrub	0.022	0.0000	Scrub	0.220	0.0000
Woodland	0.250	0.0000	Woodland	0.114	0.0001
Orange-crowned warbler			*Spotted towhee*		
Bare	0.000	0.0000	Bare	0.000	0.0000
Bluff	0.019	0.0000	Bluff	0.000	0.0000
Chaparral	0.250	0.0000	Chaparral	0.400	0.0000
Grassland	0.106	0.0339	Grassland	0.067	0.0307
Iceplant	0.000	0.0000	Iceplant	0.000	0.0000
Pine	0.158	0.0487	Pine	0.172	0.0000
Riparian	0.157	0.0001	Riparian	0.115	0.0000
Scrub	0.129	0.1864	Scrub	0.032	0.0000
Woodland	0.182	0.0000	Woodland	0.215	0.0000
Pacific-slope flycatcher			*Rock wren*		
Bare	0.000	0.0000	Bare	0.000	0.0000
Bluff	0.000	0.0000	Bluff	0.000	0.0000
Chaparral	0.270	0.0000	Chaparral	0.302	0.0950
Grassland	0.035	0.0000	Grassland	0.045	0.0027
Iceplant	0.000	0.0000	Iceplant	0.043	0.0644
Pine	0.316	0.0000	Pine	0.086	0.5485
Riparian	0.140	0.0000	Riparian	0.400	0.0000
Scrub	0.008	0.0000	Scrub	0.073	0.0031
Woodland	0.231	0.0000	Woodland	0.050	0.0405

Habitat	*Bi*	*P*	Habitat	*Bi*	*P*
Western meadowlark					
Bare	0.038	0.0000			
Bluff	0.026	0.0000			
Chaparral	0.202	0.0001			
Grassland	0.333	0.0000			
Iceplant	0.020	0.0000			
Pine	0.134	0.4515			
Riparian	0.051	0.0000			
Scrub	0.112	0.0307			
Woodland	0.085	0.0004			

Appendix D   Island-specific Standardized Habitat Selection Ratios for 15 Species

These data allow comparison of selection by bird species of habitats on different islands. For example, Allen's hummingbirds use grasslands twice as much on San Miguel ($B_i = 0.314$) as on Santa Rosa ($B_i = 0.161$), but on the latter island they also added use of two habitats (pine and woodland) not found on San Miguel.

Habitat	ANA* Bi	ANA* P	SBI Bi	SBI P	SMI Bi	SMI P	SRI Bi	SRI P
Allen's hummingbird								
Bare								
Bluff					0.000	0.0000		
Chaparral							0.143	0.0846
Grassland					0.314	0.6919	0.161	0.5332
Iceplant								
Pine							0.207	0.5355
Riparian					0.445	0.0722	0.236	0.0153
Scrub					0.241	0.5253	0.056	0.0000
Woodland							0.198	0.6359
Anna's hummingbird								
Bare								
Bluff								
Chaparral							0.165	0.9658
Grassland							0.115	0.4293
Iceplant								
Pine							0.230	0.2460
Riparian							0.115	0.0606
Scrub							0.173	0.9274
Woodland							0.202	0.3394
Bewick's wren								
Bare								
Bluff								
Chaparral							0.191	0.3159
Grassland	0.128	0.0000					0.181	0.8096
Iceplant	0.154	0.0113						
Pine							0.131	0.0005
Riparian							0.215	0.0001
Scrub	0.718	0.0000					0.116	0.0003
Woodland							0.165	0.2854

*ANI = Anacapa Island, SBI = Santa Barbara Island, SMI = San Miguel Island, SRI = Santa Rosa Island

	ANI		SBI		SMI		SRI	
Habitat	*Bi*	*P*	*Bi*	*P*	*Bi*	*P*	*Bi*	*P*
Black phoebe								
Bare								
Bluff								
Chaparral							0.023	0.0000
Grassland							0.272	0.4843
Iceplant								
Pine							0.023	0.0000
Riparian							0.478	0.0000
Scrub							0.163	0.7238
Woodland							0.041	0.0000
California quail								
Bare								
Bluff								
Chaparral							0.195	0.3288
Grassland							0.260	0.2015
Iceplant								
Pine							0.125	0.5380
Riparian							0.153	0.8879
Scrub							0.170	0.7284
Woodland							0.097	0.0436
Chipping sparrow								
Bare								
Bluff								
Chaparral							0.104	0.1385
Grassland							0.353	0.0000
Iceplant								
Pine							0.144	0.0465
Riparian							0.064	0.0000
Scrub							0.261	0.0000
Woodland							0.074	0.0000
House finch								
Bare								
Bluff						0.000	0.0000		
Chaparral							0.145	0.5332
Grassland					0.627	0.1707	0.204	0.0545
Iceplant								
Pine							0.193	0.0115
Riparian					0.086	0.0406	0.140	0.1111
Scrub					0.287	0.5047	0.191	0.0842
Woodland							0.127	0.0058

Habitat	ANI Bi	P	SBI Bi	P	SMI Bi	P	SRI Bi	P
Horned lark								
Bare			0.041	0.0000				
Bluff			0.063	0.0001	0.079	0.0000		
Chaparral							0.013	0.0000
Grassland			0.631	0.0000	0.650	0.0000	0.803	0.0000
Iceplant			0.180	0.9512				
Pine							0.083	0.9911
Riparian					0.017	0.0000	0.019	0.0000
Scrub			0.084	0.0000	0.254	0.1506	0.056	0.2682
Woodland							0.026	0.0000
Lesser goldfinch								
Bare								
Bluff								
Chaparral							0.193	0.0279
Grassland							0.226	0.0349
Iceplant								
Pine							0.151	0.7909
Riparian							0.088	0.0000
Scrub							0.196	0.0996
Woodland							0.146	0.9713
Orange-crowned warbler								
Bare			0.000	0.0000				
Bluff			0.116	0.0299	0.063	0.0000		
Chaparral							0.174	0.2131
Grassland			0.421	0.1386	0.404	0.0652	0.206	0.0450
Iceplant			0.000	0.0000				
Pine							0.110	0.0001
Riparian					0.131	0.0000	0.167	0.2045
Scrub			0.463	0.0000	0.402	0.0000	0.217	0.0052
Woodland							0.126	0.0012
Pacific-slope flycatcher								
Bare								
Bluff								
Chaparral							0.190	0.3903
Grassland							0.166	0.8119
Iceplant								
Pine							0.223	0.0191
Riparian							0.175	0.8736
Scrub							0.084	0.0000
Woodland							0.163	0.4486

Habitat	ANI Bi	ANI P	SBI Bi	SBI P	SMI Bi	SMI P	SRI Bi	SRI P
Rock wren								
Bare								
Bluff								
Chaparral							0.188	0.9038
Grassland							0.188	0.9401
Iceplant								
Pine							0.054	0.0001
Riparian							0.444	0.0000
Scrub							0.094	0.1172
Woodland							0.031	0.0000
Song sparrow								
Bare								
Bluff					0.104	0.0000		
Chaparral							0.088	0.0004
Grassland					0.450	0.0001	0.356	0.0000
Iceplant								
Pine							0.022	0.0000
Riparian					0.051	0.0000	0.132	0.1659
Scrub					0.395	0.0000	0.347	0.0000
Woodland							0.055	0.0000
Spotted towhee								
Bare								
Bluff								
Chaparral							0.209	0.0000
Grassland							0.231	0.0002
Iceplant								
Pine							0.089	0.0000
Riparian							0.106	0.0000
Scrub							0.253	0.0000
Woodland							0.112	0.0003
Western meadowlark								
Bare			0.080	0.0000				
Bluff			0.066	0.0000	0.055	0.0000		
Chaparral							0.099	0.6629
Grassland			0.640	0.0000	0.759	0.0000	0.412	0.0000
Iceplant			0.059	0.0000				
Pine							0.065	0.0000
Riparian					0.010	0.0000	0.042	0.0000
Scrub			0.155	0.0001	0.176	0.0716	0.341	0.0000
Woodland							0.041	0.0000

Appendix E   Island-specific Habitat Selection Profiles for 15 Species

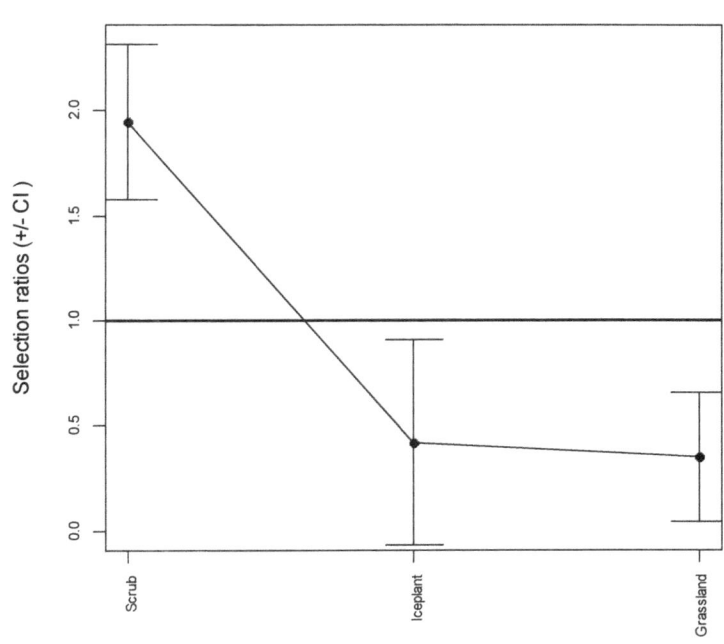

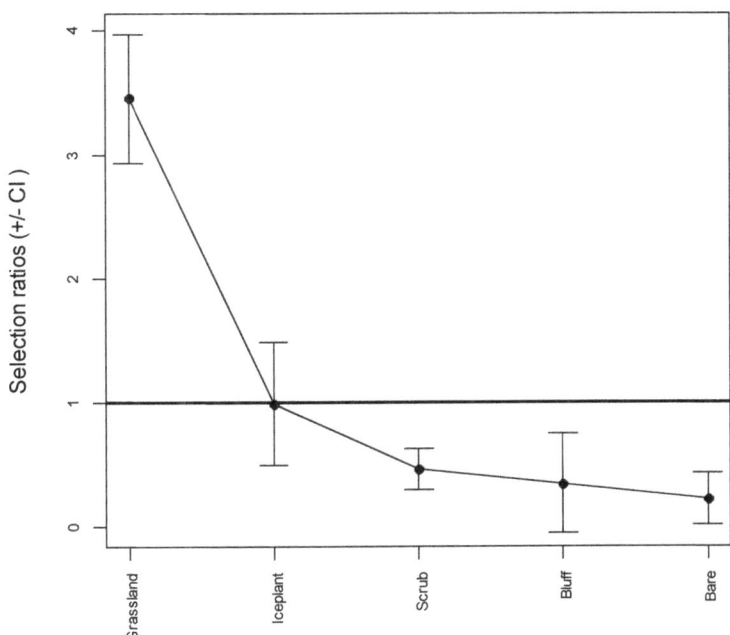

Orange-crowned Warbler - SBI

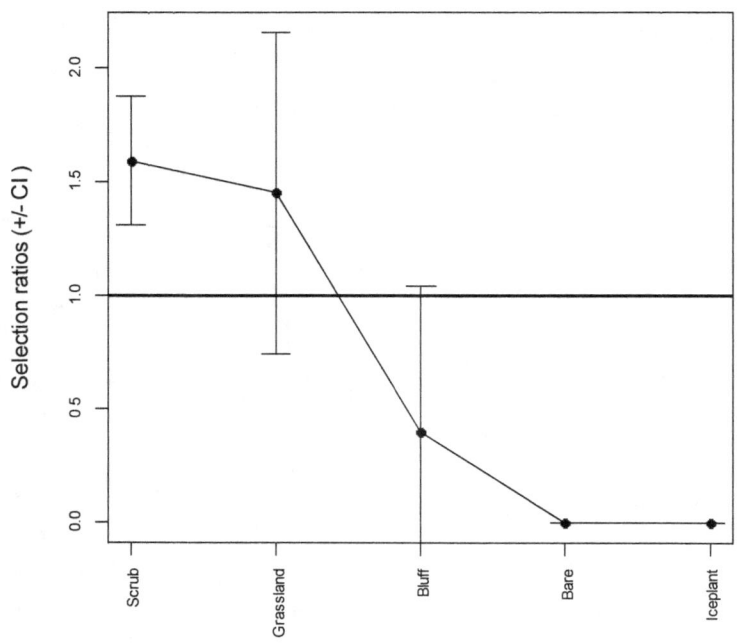

Western Meadowlark - SBI

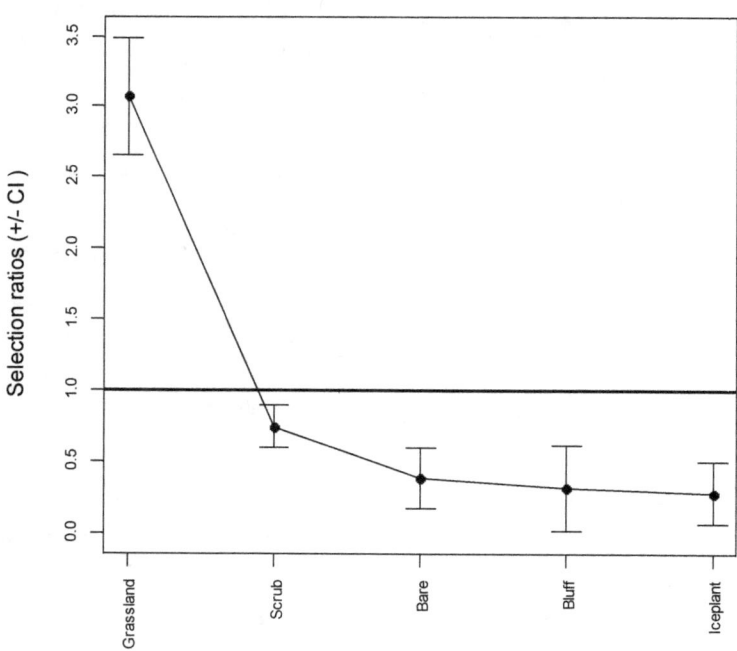

Allen's Hummingbird - SMI

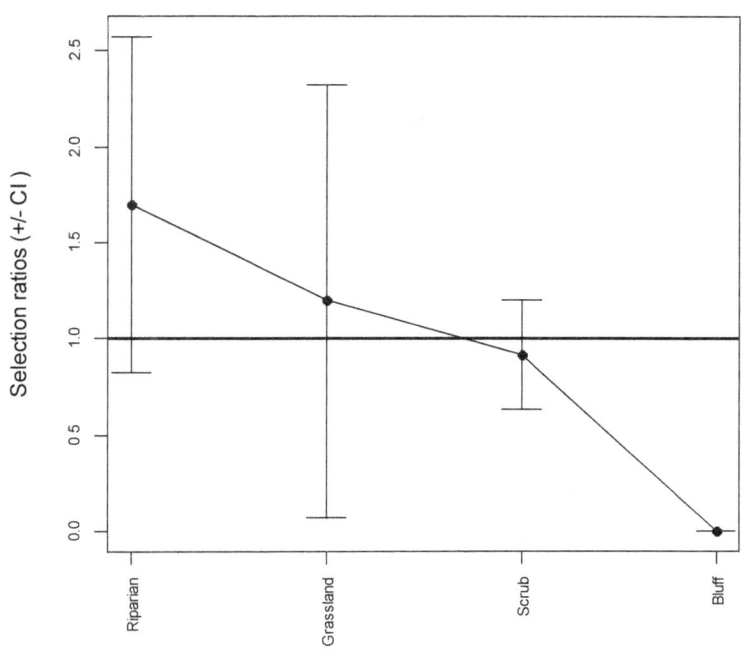

House Finch - SMI

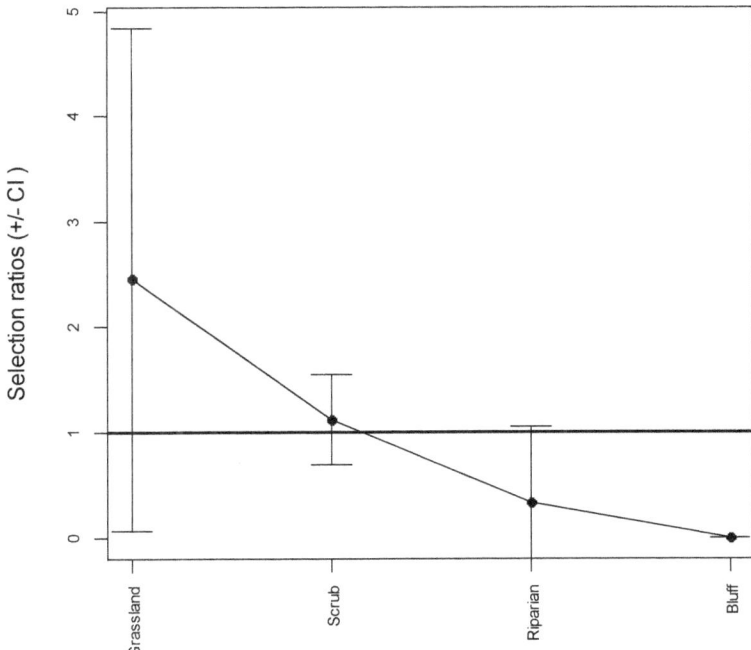

Horned Lark - SMI

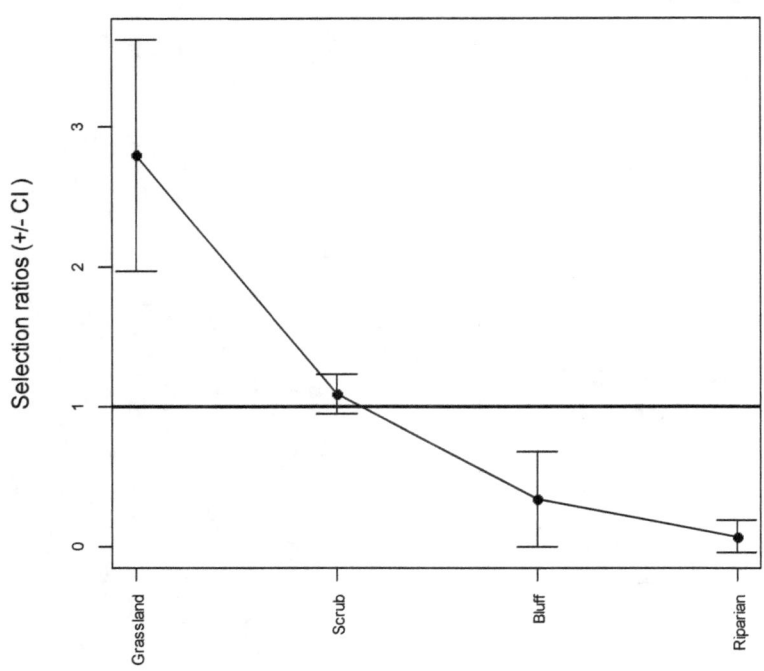

Orange-crowned Warbler - SMI

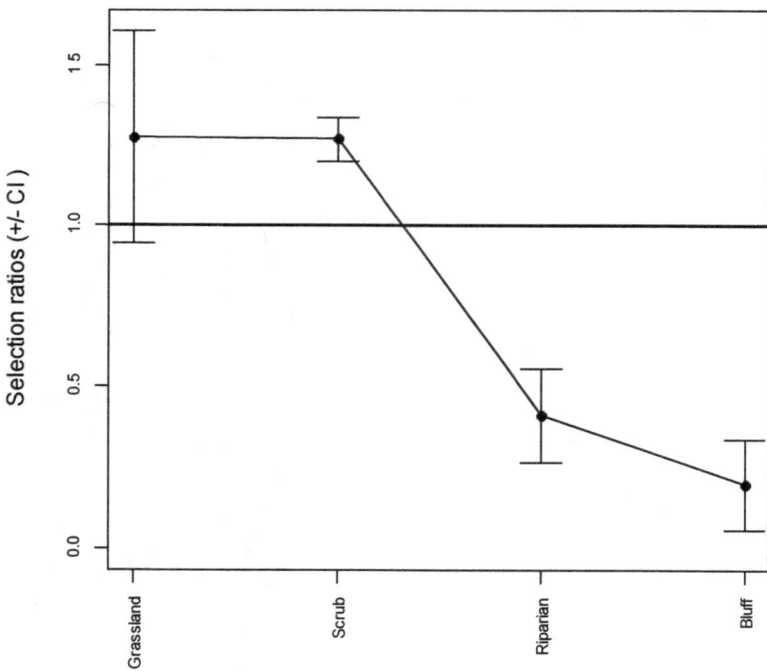

Song Sparrow - SMI

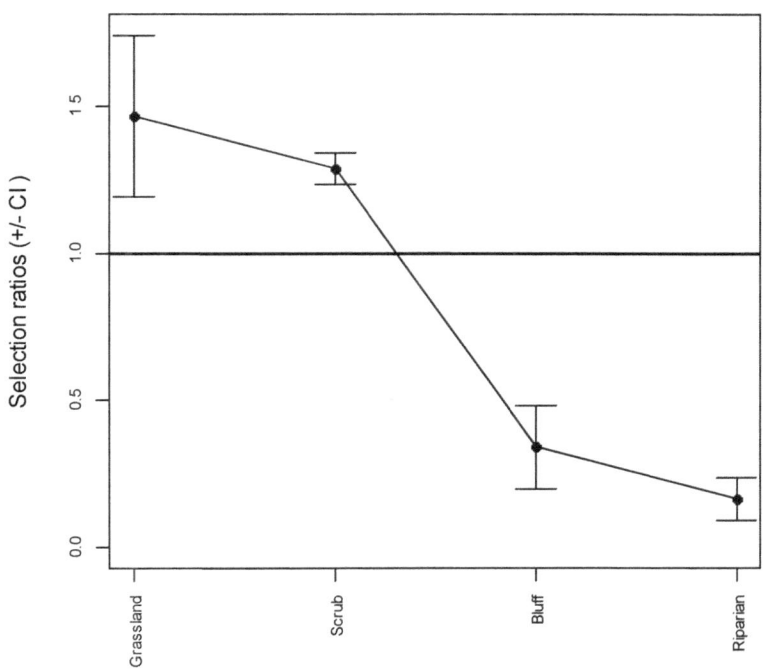

Western Meadowlark - SMI

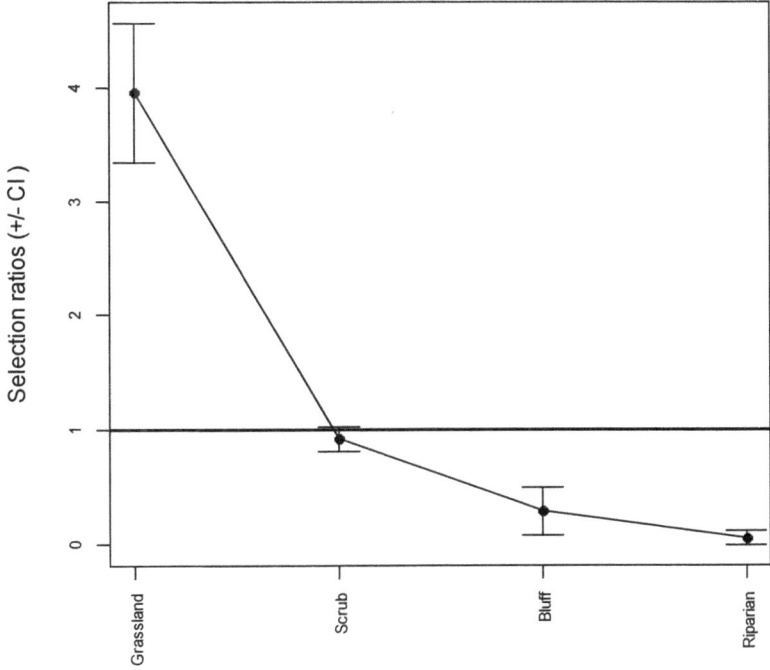

Allen's Hummingbird - SRI

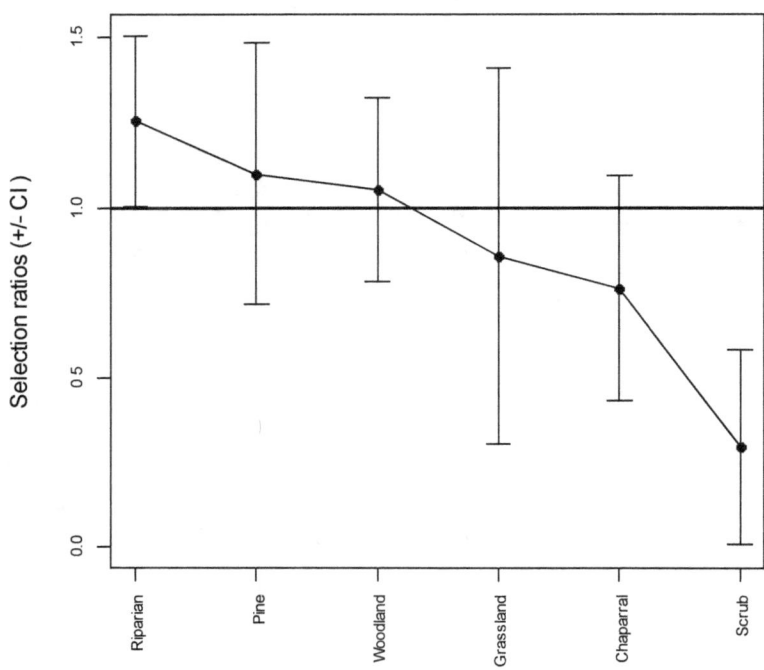

Anna's Hummingbird - SRI

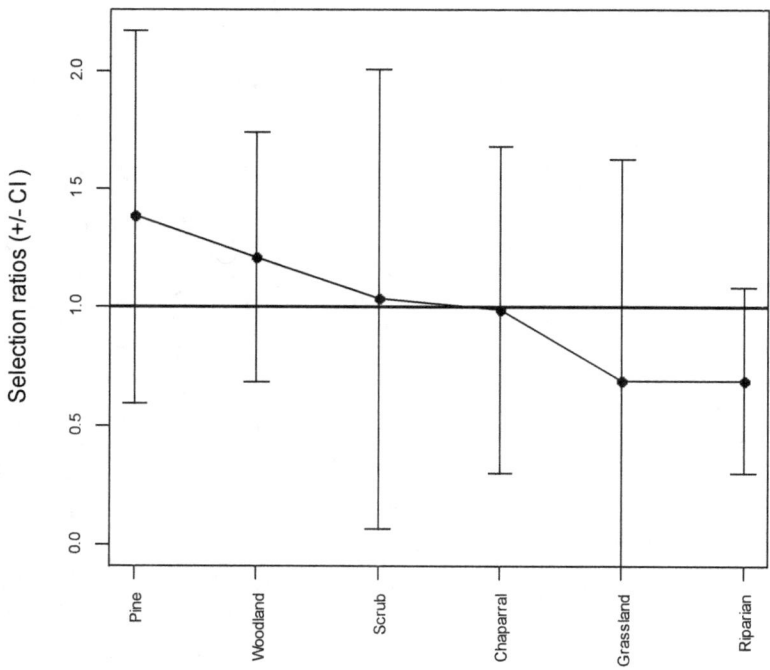

Bewick's Wren - SRI

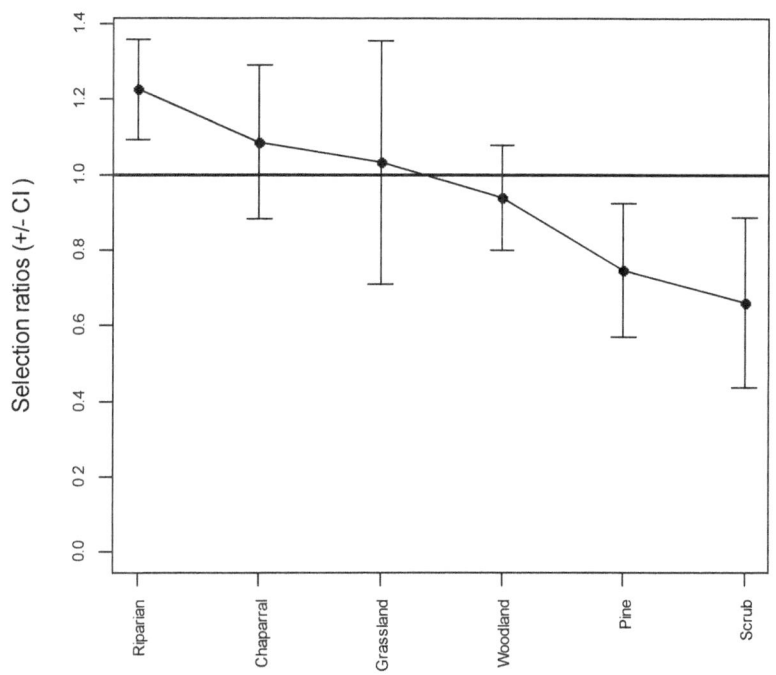

Black Phoebe - SRI

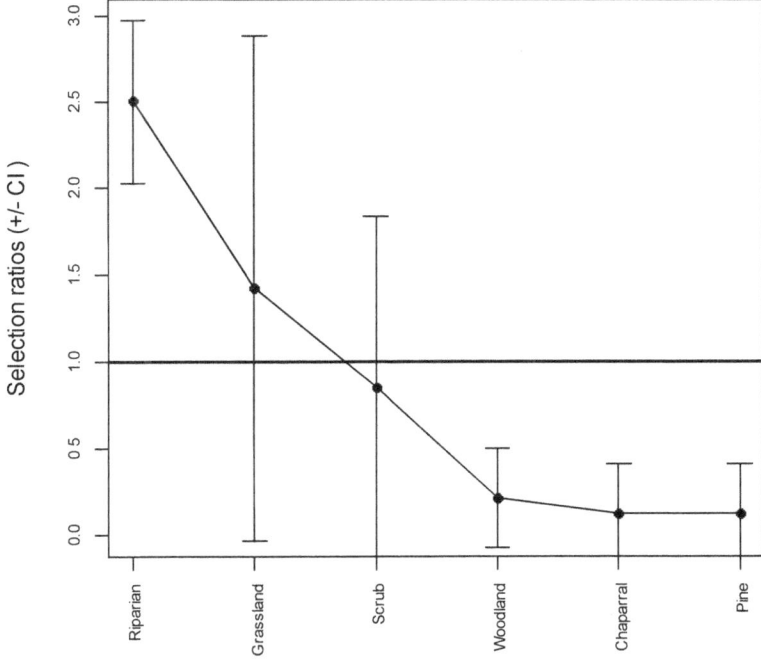

California Quail - SRI

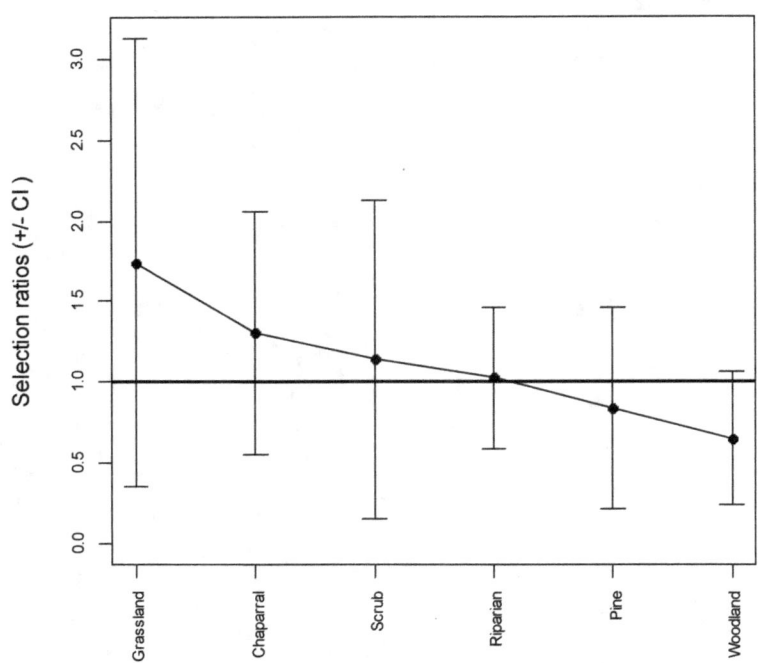

Chipping Sparrow - SRI

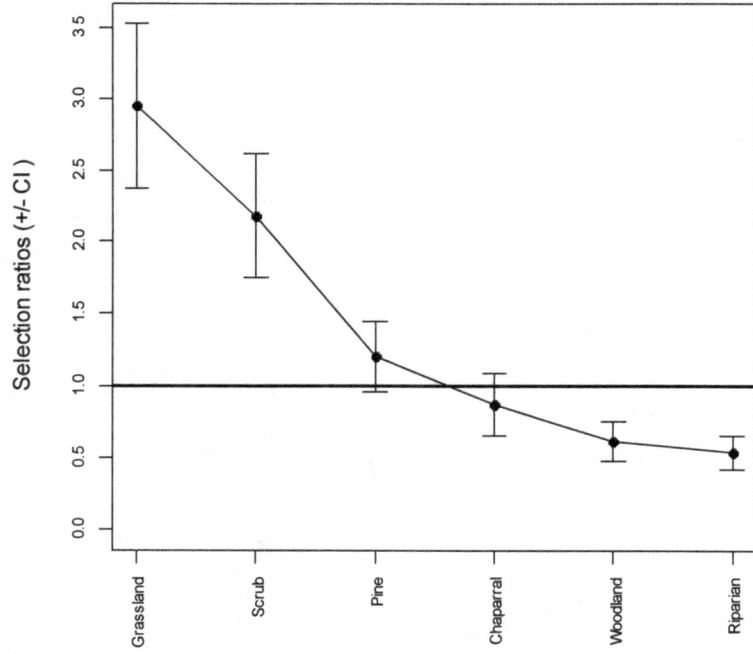

80

House Finch - SRI

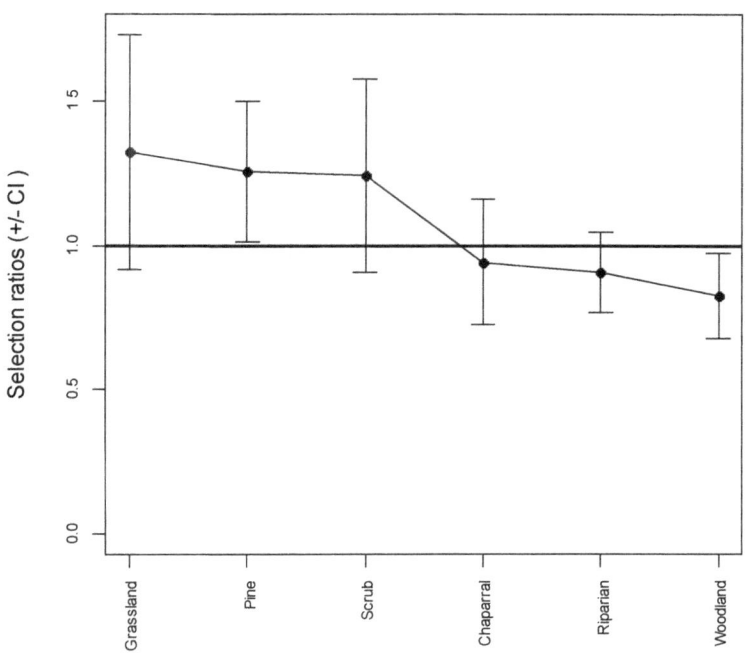

Horned Lark - SRI

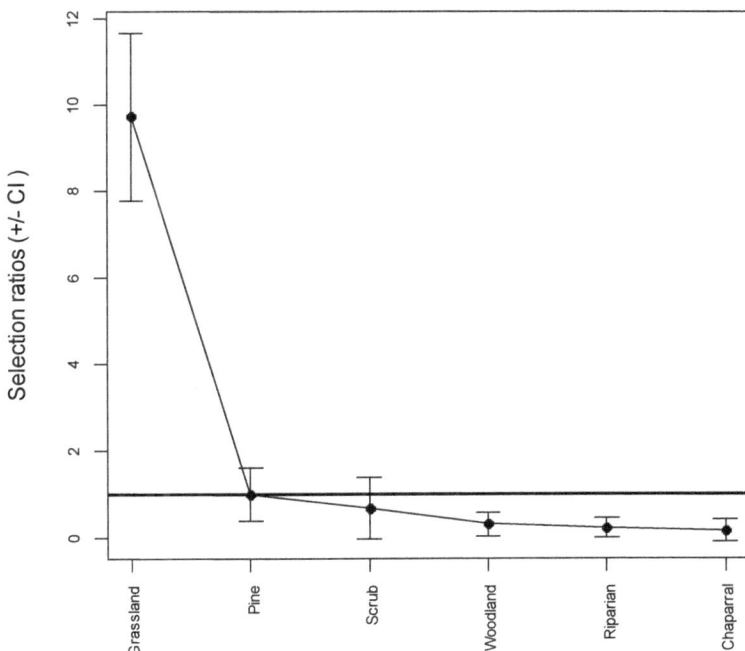

81

Lesser Goldfinch - SRI

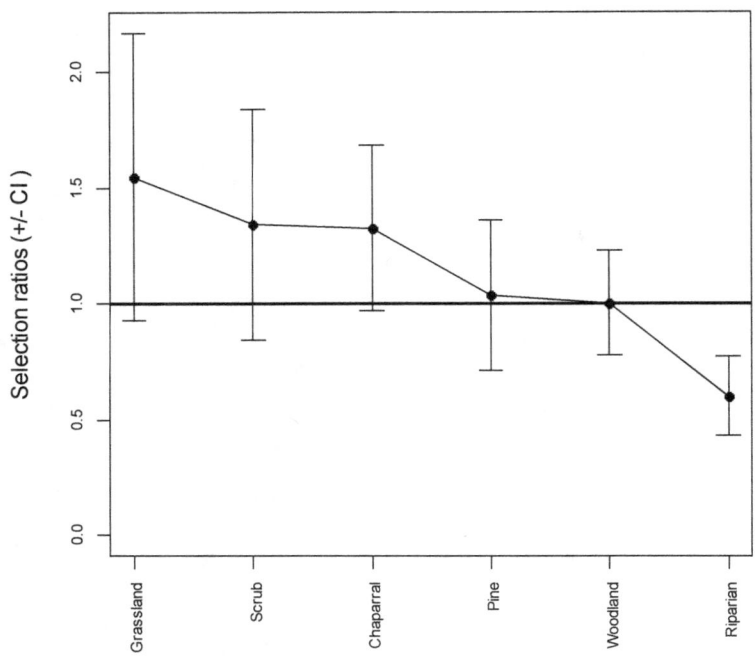

Orange-crowned Warbler - SRI

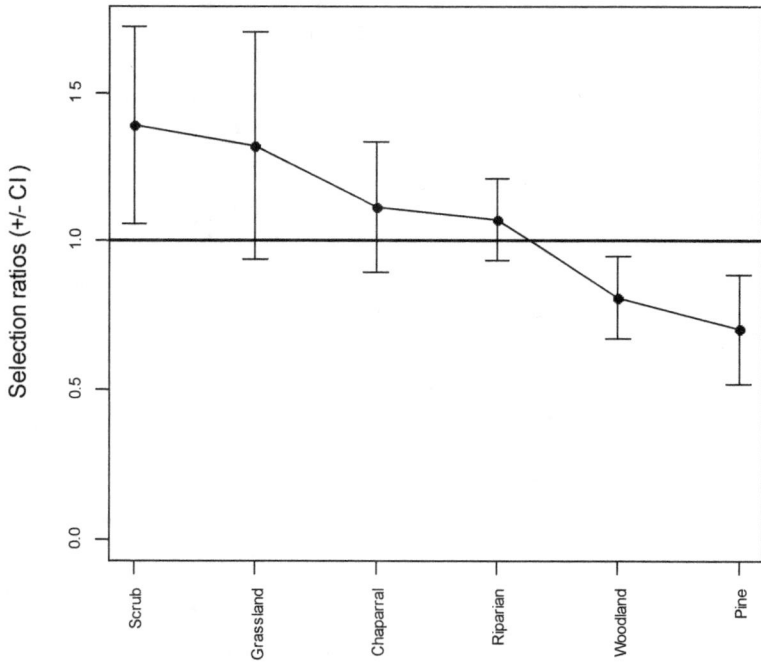

Pacific-slope Flycatcher - SRI

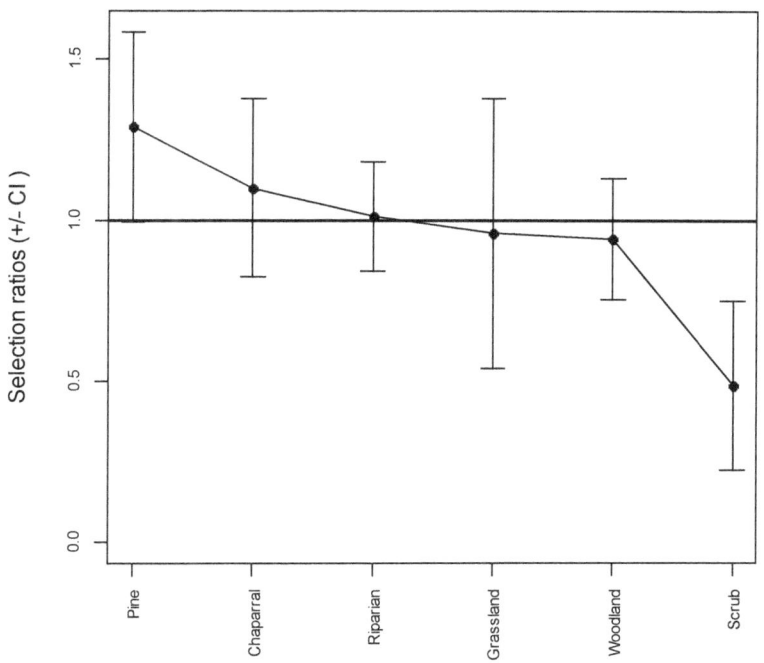

Rock Wren - SRI

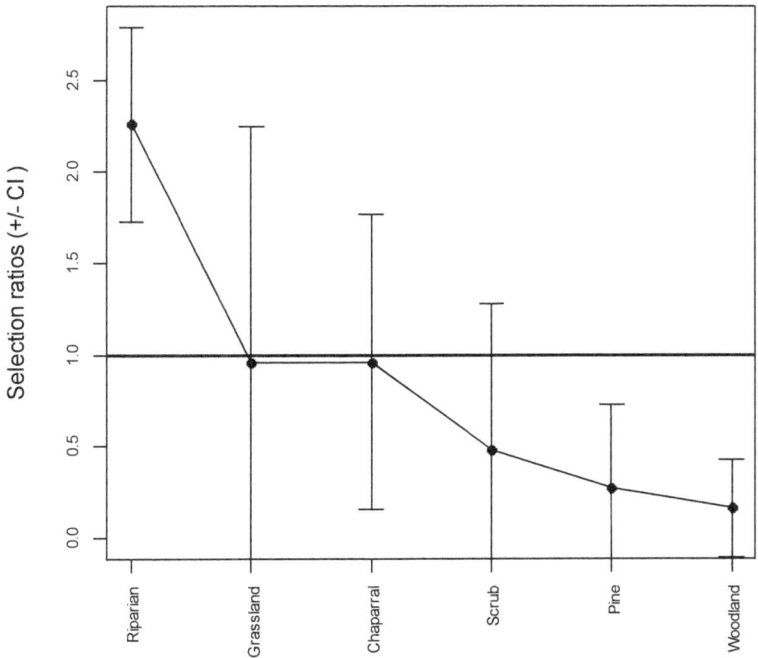

Song Sparrow - SRI

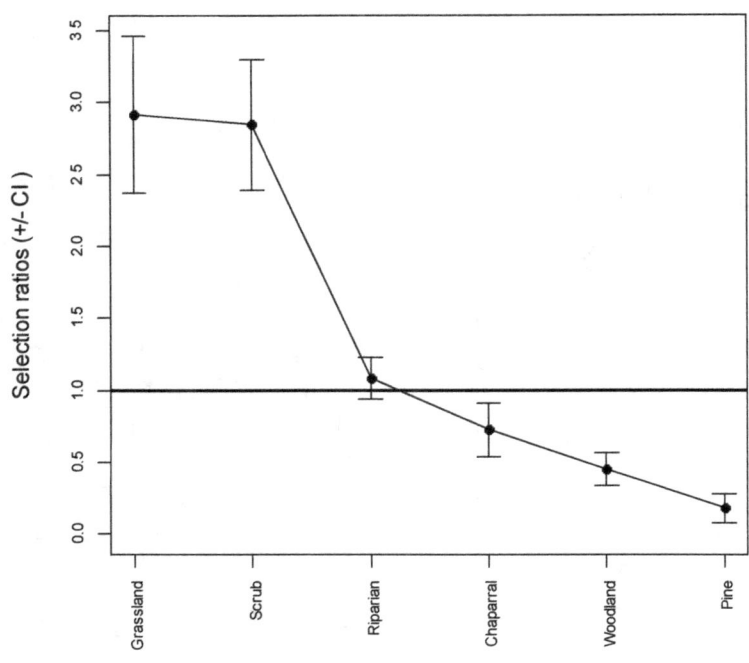

Spotted Towhee - SRI

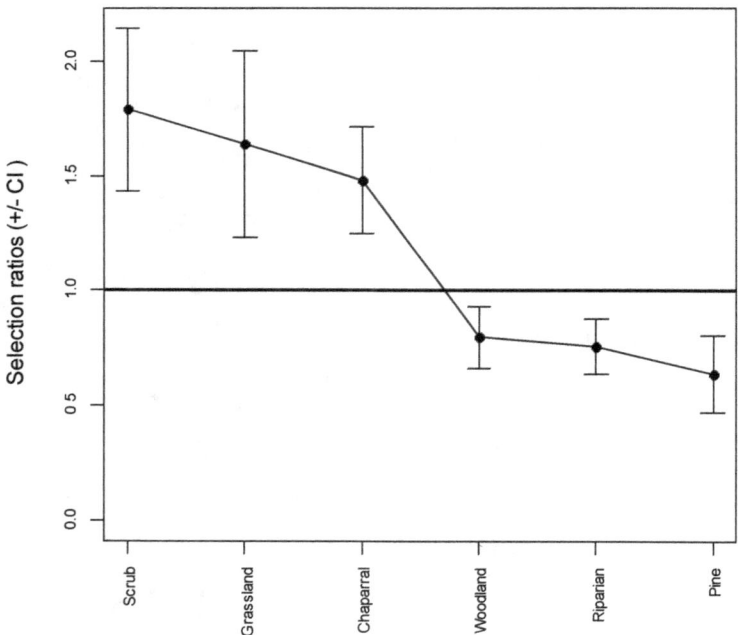

84

Western Meadowlark - SRI

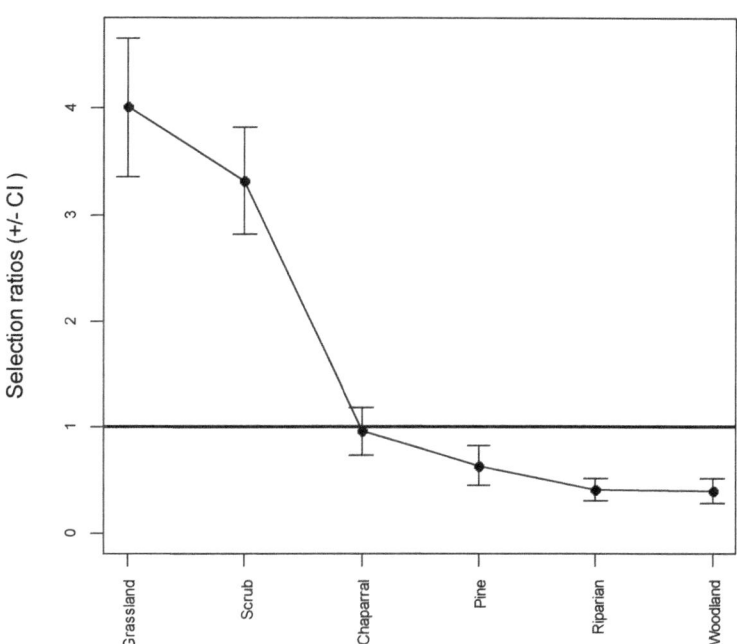

NPS 159/111616, November 2011

www.ingramcontent.com/pod-product-compliance
Lightning Source LLC
Chambersburg PA
CBHW080315290526
45790CB00005B/2045